Making Church Buildings Work

Revd Maggie Durran, after several years as a vicar on the Old Kent Road in Walworth, South London, began to exercise her gifts and ministry in working with churches all over London on their buildings. For the past five years, as part-time historic churches project officer for the Diocese of London and as a freelance development and fundraising consultant she has worked with churches with building problems of many kinds. The result is a keen perspective of the challenges of church buildings and a wide experience of good management practice and the problem-solving solutions adopted in a variety of churches.

Making Church Buildings Work

A handbook for managing and developing church buildings for mission and ministry

Maggie Durran

CANTERBURY
PRESS
Norwich

First published in 2005 by the Canterbury Press Norwich
(a publishing imprint of Hymns Ancient & Modern Limited,
a registered charity)
St Mary's Works, St Mary's Plain,
Norwich, Norfolk, NR3 3BH

www.scm-canterburypress.co.uk

British Library Cataloguing in Publication data

A catalogue record for this book is available
from the British Library

ISBN 1-85311-597-5

Typeset by Regent Typesetting
Printed and bound in Great Britain by
William Clowes Ltd, Beccles, Suffolk

Contents

Part 1 Introduction   **1**

1 Introduction   3
2 Rediscovering the Church Building Story   8
3 The Church's Mission   13

Part 2 Managing Your Building   **21**

4 Health and Safety   23
5 Increasing Access   33
6 Maintenance   36
7 Repair   43
8 Faculty Jurisdiction and the Diocesan
   Advisory Committee   52
9 Change of Use and Additional Uses   56
10 Running New Uses   66
11 Letting or Leasing the Church or Hall   71
12 Community Projects and their Sustainability   82
13 Visitors   86

Part 3 Major Building Projects   **93**

14 Preparing for Major Building Projects   95
   What is the need?   95

Developing the brief   100
Managing the project   103
The architect and the design team   105
Legal consents   110
Processing funds   111
Detailed design and tendering   112
Practical completion   115
Look out! Potential problems   115

15 Managing People and Buildings   125
    New uses   125
    Leadership   128
    People   132
    Responsibilities of being an employer   135

Appendices
    1 Risk Analysis Chart   145
    2 Chart for Schedule and Brief Preparation   146
    3 Church Hall Handbook   150
    4 Elements of a Contract of Employment   162

Resources   164

Index   167

Part 1

Introduction

1

Introduction

When I first took responsibility for a church building my knowledge was minimal, my experience even less and only the recollection from my childhood of my father's good-sense management skills saved my bacon and the building's. I would have liked some information, such as that which follows, in a straightforward manner, to fill in the gaps – many of which I fell headlong into at some time or other. Yet I have spent much of my working time in the past 15 years dealing with buildings, their repairs and adaptations, their use and their maintenance. On the way some pretty good building professionals have helped me find my feet and a very few bad ones have given me a good idea of some problems to avoid. So this book serves as an introduction to the good points that a lot of really helpful people have enabled me add to my repertoire.

The changes in the way we use church buildings for liturgy for contemporary worship result in a need for reordering. Add to that the facilities that contemporary congregations find to be essential, from toilets to heating, induction loops and PA systems, and already many churches face an enormous challenge to effect change. The great dilemmas of finding a change that suits current use and suits the other stakeholders – the Diocesan Advisory Committee and the faculty process, English Heritage and the Victorian Society – can be eased by a systematic process. Many church councils get frustrated after trying to plan changes to the building and getting their plans rejected by outside authorities. The work of preparing a brief (starting on p. 100), and then meeting the church architect who understands the heritage demands and who can interface those creatively with the functional needs of the church, is the productive way forward.

In a difficult financial climate, in the process of finding ways to make our buildings sustainable – that is, to find ways to pay for repairs and maintenance so the building is there for future generations – many churches seek to establish additional uses in their building, so it can earn its living every day and not just on Sundays. Beginning with a local audit of potential community and commercial demand for build-ing space is the solid foundation that feeds into a good feasibility study on the architectural way to meet those needs. This combination – of preparing a good brief for the architect and a good presentation on how those needs may be met within the limitations of the building – forms an excellent basis for dialogue with the statutory authorities. Both these steps can also contribute to a business plan that substanti-ates the programme for potential funders of a capital construction programme.

The goalposts are constantly moving on the legally required safe-guards in using a church building. High on the horizon at present are health and safety, access and the risk analysis. Most churches have in the past proceeded on the basis of common sense about the safety of their buildings and the people who use or work in them. However, the usual benchmark will be an 'industry standard'. As more churches introduce various programmes into their buildings the standard of safety care they set will increasingly become the standard for all churches. Why? Insurance is the short answer. Where the churches with better safety policies and actions are having fewer accidents or less harassment or attacks on clergy and other staff, there will be an increased requirement for all churches to address health and safety more thoroughly. The Disability Access Audit required by law by 2004 in all public buildings means that every church should have undertaken an audit and then have taken reasonable action to adapt to their audit's requirements. In Chapter 5 this audit is taken several steps further as those of us with significant heritage buildings in our care can address the access needs of many others of our visitors or potential visitors in considering intellectual, language and cultural barriers to access to our church.

What is at stake if your church building leaks in water from time to time? Is it enough to ensure that there is a bucket underneath or to assume that the heating system dries up the residue? Only recently I found out how 'fruiting bodies' or mushroom-like growths appear where water has crept in under the roof materials and eaten into the wood; all too soon large areas of roof become damaged and dangerous. It has become obvious over more years that many churches would be saved vast repair bills if regular minor maintenance programmes were enacted. Top of the list would be cleaning the gutters several times each year as blocked gutters are the most likely instigators of water ingress. Following closely behind are weeds and vegetation in the wrong places and slipped tiles/slates. Once the wind and rain find a little corner to access they eat away at the structure and major repairs are soon needed. The maintenance programme in Chapter 6 is a starting-point. A few hours spent three or four times each year will save a huge effort of construction (and fundraising) to deal with a major problem.

Each church, as part of the legal measure that keeps churches outside the listed building concern of the local authority, has to have a five-yearly inspection, leading to the quinquennial report. This is a long enough cycle to allow major repairs or failures in maintenance to come to light. The standard format is for the inspecting architect (paid for and employed by the diocese) to inspect and report on the general condition of the building and to highlight repair needs, categorizing them as immediately needed, needed within two years or needed within the five-year cycle. Having a strategy for maintenance and repair will make the reports more productive and useful to the local church.

Seeing major repairs through from start to finish, from identifying the need and engaging the architect to commissioning and completing the work, is the subject of Chapter 14. Understanding good practice in employing building professionals, knowing who is likely to be doing what and when, and especially who is going to control the budget and cost of the work, not only reduces stress but helps the church get the outcome they both wanted and needed. Many of the major catastrophes of church building and repair programmes are caused by the client/church not knowing what to do and how to keep the whole process under control. Just a few potential catastrophes are outlined on p. 115, and most can be avoided by following a good process.

Gaining permission from the relevant internal and external authorities is the protective system that safeguards the interests of future generations of the church as well as accommodating the concerns of the heritage bodies. For historic churches this process includes consulting societies such as the Georgian and Victorian societies where relevant.

Understanding the process and using the skills of a good architect to design changes to the building will make the whole process easier though maybe no shorter. (See page 46 on how to change your architect.) The church council is well placed to prepare a statement of their need for change and a brief about the functional changes, but the architect designing for change to meet these needs will know the way through the permissions network.

All too often churches consider change and additional uses in the church or church hall without considering two key elements: What is the sustainability of the new project once the capital works are complete? In other words, is it financially viable, or will it impact negatively on church finance? And what are the management or staff implications of the new project as it progresses? These questions are tackled in lots of ways throughout the book. In Chapter 11 the issues of letting or leasing the church hall are covered. Community projects in church premises and run by church members are explored in Chapter 12, as again many church councils get as far as planning the construction or setting up of the project without fully exploring how the project will be maintained and sustained in the longer term.

When we change our buildings from Sunday-only churches to everyday churches not only does this change the maintenance need, but almost always there are changes in management and staffing. While the chapters on managing people are not comprehensive, they do introduce the reader to many of the issues and principles involved in engaging paid staff and volunteers to work in the church. Staff may be caring for the building, supervising its use or looking after visitors. Many aspects from recruitment to staff meetings and team-building are explored. How the team co-operates in making all things work together for good is critical to new and extended uses in church buildings. Those churches establishing specialist welfare and similar projects that require professional workers and professional supervision will want to ensure additional skills are brought into management. And those who read these chapters will be regularly reminded to gain the necessary permission for their activity and to ensure they have the appropriate insurance.

Probably we all want more visitors in our churches. But if we are open to drop-in visitors we have the responsibility of ensuring the standard of care is at least reasonable and that the provision for visitors enables them to benefit from their visit. They may not want to know what we first want to tell them, and their motivation in visiting may be different from ours. Chapter 13 suggests many ways of catering for the needs of visitors. It also encompasses consideration of when those people visiting church are less than positive and safety and security are issues. There are suggestions on attracting new visitors and enabling them to cross the cultural divide that may be the result of language, ethnicity, faith or age, or all of them!

The practical issues are where this book starts and ends. However, Chapter 3 introduces some principles, theological and social, that help us keep a constructive and positive viewpoint as we tackle issues and work programmes that beset us with tasks around the church. We will be encouraged to see the building as another part of Christian witness, as a factor for good in our evangelism and of itself a record of the story of the Christian faith journey and witness in the neighbourhood. It's about why we need our church buildings, and how the effort of keeping them looking beautiful and functioning well is a productive part of our mission.

2

Rediscovering the Church Building Story

Many threads, positive and negative, are drawn together in our consideration of our church buildings.[1] They are undoubtedly public buildings, with a binding responsibility for key functions in our national and individual lives. The parochial system ensures that every resident has access for weddings, funerals and baptisms as well as to public worship. Yet churches are not financed by anyone other than those who regularly attend, a minority of local residents. Neither inherently good or bad as a system, as long as it works well we may even enjoy it, but when problems arise, we may well resent the responsibilities for maintaining expensive, historic buildings.

When such a system, somewhat antiquated maybe, is set in today's market economy, the timbers creak and the sails often billow sadly. Without a collective sense of local responsibility from parish residents, the parochial system that undergirds the current legal and financial structure, we often need to seek new ways within that market to make our churches viable; we become entrepreneurial and put them to multi-purpose use. There is nothing wrong with this when we keep focused on our mission as churches and give careful regard to our history and to our context and keep in mind future generations of the church.

Churches throughout history have been interpretative of the faith of those who built them; not just their architects but their congregations too. The great Arts and Crafts Church of St Cuthbert's, Philbeach Gardens, in London, is lined with clay tiles, individually crafted by

---

1 Drawing on threads from a talk by Bishop Richard Chartres at the OUCH conference, 18 November 2003.

members of the congregation who returned each Sunday with tiles in hand for the next stage of decoration. Here, faith is interpreted in the building style, finish and content.

In medieval churches the vision of God as distant and numinous was interpreted into the distant table and reredos, with chancel arch and screen, often hiding the celebration of the Mass from the common people. In later renditions of this form more and more steps were added to the long journey from the font at the back of the nave to the chancel and choir and then highest of all the table and reredos. People and priests approached with awe. It was a style that lent itself to dignified procession and high ritual embodying the sense of the greatness and otherness of God.

The later churches of the Reformers and Cranmer were communitarian, the people facing each other, with the communion table in the centre or, as in the early St Paul's Cathedral, in the east end. The shape reflected the call for community, for drawing together the fragmented and building up the body of Christ.

Added to these patterns – the long-aisled medieval and neo-Gothic and the more square and communitarian – are the foci of worship: the font near the entrance, the pulpit for the presentation of the word, the desk for the clerk or president and the table for the communion. The placing of each reflects again the interrelationship between people and God and each other. It amplifies the theology of priesthood among the contemporary congregation.

In our present age there are great movements in liturgy and worship. Focus for many is not just on the numinous but also on the immanence more than the transcendence of God. And in the wide spectrum of current patterns of worship, whether maintaining the Anglo-Catholic (often in Victorian neo-Gothic cathedral-sized parish churches) or establishing a charismatic community of the gathered church, diversity and change are rife.

Very often a congregation in flux with regard to its forms of worship, liturgy and perceptions of God is also in flux interpreting that developing faith in the building in which it finds itself. Often it seems a misfit, and our parochial system holds the congregation in an apparent anachronism of a building that does not fit easily to its new style.

Change is not easy. Can a church with long flowing arched aisles of the nave leading to the distant altar be altered for the congregation to face each other with the priest among them? It is not as simple as finding the money to alter or rebuild. There are obvious problems, these buildings are national treasures, public buildings in semi-private ownership, protected from change by the system of listing and faculty jurisdiction. One common reason for seeking change is the running cost of huge buildings – monsters – when the worshipping community may be very few and ageing. Yet replacement would be extremely costly. 'I am walking underneath an elephant and I'm afraid it may sit down'; a church building may be an extremely threatening burden.

But there are more subtle and perhaps richer reasons too for avoiding wholesale change. Our church buildings carry the story of the faith journey of God's people through many generations. Our particular contemporary interpretation of our faith and how that might be expressed in our building is just one generation in a story of many generations, each inheriting and building on the gifts and strengths of those who went before, and always looking forward to those who will come in the future. Our present generation has little grasp of the responsibility to the future church, and this is probably tied to our contemporary sense of powerlessness in the face of potential nuclear holocaust or global warming catastrophe. But that might be mirrored by the early Church's sense that the second coming was about to whisk them away or that they might be destroyed by the mighty power of Rome through persecution and the holocaust of the gladiators fighting to the death.

But on reflection our buildings, bearing the faith of many generations of Christians before us, have a story to tell. They are like the stone altars that Abraham constructed on his journey to the Promised Land: named 'Ebenezer, for thus far has the Lord brought us'. Whether we read the tiles of St Cuthbert's or the church council minutes of the early 1800s to know why these pews were installed or the organ loft placed just so, we enter just a little into the faith that has paved our way. For many even very old buildings, records exist of the architect's original design, of the congregation's concerns, the struggle to raise the funds and the arduous work of building.

As we consider change and development, it will enrich our own faith journey if we discover and contemplate the work of the builders and furnishers of our churches, grapple with their interpretation of God in building form and then seek to add our layer, not to annihilate theirs. We will consider not just the needs and perceptions of our congregation but also the role our public building plays for our local community, who may not be churchgoers or may be of another faith, and its role as a service to them, its place in the local environment and its embodiment of local faith and community over many generations.

Interpreting the principles

Where does this take us if our church is a monster, seemingly impossible to maintain or appropriately change, if its form is arguing with the community of the body of Christ we seek to establish? The aisles and pews may not enhance the free-flowing easygoing worship we are developing, and the high and distant altar takes the priest to a status we do not believe in.

What are the issues we find? They are issues to explore in contemporary theology. What is our view of God, and of how worship and liturgy fit for our contemporary congregation *and for the communities that surround us*? We may actually be seeking a more open and accessible form of worship that our unchurched neighbours can step into, where contemporary language and values can find their place. Is the priest the only one to enter that high and numinous place, or in the days of equal opportunities do we want to find the priests down among us, and their role less 'other' and more as one of us serving on our behalf?

We can gather the story of our church, not just its architectural history, but also its faith journey, and retell its story so it becomes alive to us. Maybe we can create a photographic record of features that remain and add the recollections of our oldest members and the changes they have seen. Collect together the generations of photographs of churchgoers, staff and local people and rediscover the story.

Consider thoroughly the changing face of the vicar's ministry to the parish, and not just to church members. Very often we find ourselves saying parish when we mean church members because we have forgotten that our clergy are charged with the care of everyone who lives in our geographical parish. Many clergy now seek to have a church office for meeting people and use the study in their homes for more private work. Their families are less 'the vicarage family', and often spouses have a job of their own and other foci to their lives. Security and recent increases in violence against clergy result in them seeking to create an office near where others work – for safety – and not to carry that threat into the family home. Carving the clergy office and the administrator's office out of a rectangular worship space without damaging the integrity of the worship space requires ingenuity and skilful design.

As churches and church halls are used increasingly on an everyday basis for a variety of activities for local people, the changes can be more significant. To protect the heritage, changes may need to be reversible and taken with consideration for the long term, but innovation abounds.

A pattern of preparation, covered in the chapter which follows, encourages every church to start its consideration of its building with a look at the building's own story – its significance to members and past members, to local people and residents of former days. It also suggests that the first stage of development and the key to good managements is the church's own vision for worship, mission and ministry. Only as we gather who we are, how we see and worship God, how we relate to our neighbours and how we seek to reach out in God's name will we know how to interpret the most contemporary of faith journeys into our buildings that have reflected and interpreted the faith of the generations of Christians who stewarded and handed on this gift – or this monster – to us.

3

The Church's Mission

To where are you travelling?

A church that has no sense of forward movement will go nowhere. As the church identifies the elements of its journey, its unique sense of calling to worship, mission and service, a growing sense will emerge about how that journey and sense of God is best interpreted in the church building and how the building may best be used or adapted to the needs of mission.

The challenges

Find out, through enquiries to local residents, the value placed on the church by local people.

For example:

'Is the St ___ Church important in this community's life?'

'Are there activities that you or your family take part in at church?'

'Were any of your family baptized (christened), married or buried there?'

'If the church disappeared would this leave a gap in your life or in your environment?'

'Do you think local children should grow up knowing about the church's history?'

'Are you aware of how long the church has been here? Do you know in what ways it has traditionally served local people?'

'Are there activities or facilities you would like the church to provide, or think it should provide?'

'Are there members of your wider family who would like to be baptized or married in the church?'

Find out the Christian story of the church

Look through old registers, photos, old church council minutes and find out the issues that have concerned people in the past. Look for references, for example, to the two world wars, the 1930s Depression, at previous efforts at major repair and refurbishment. Consider modern redevelopment and the impact that has had on the neighbourhood.

Collect together the church stories of the oldest members and share them together with the other history finds.

Discover the stories of local families, where they lived and their records in the church. Can you piece together elements of their involvement with the church?

Find out about the architectural history

Find out about the original architect, and who has served as inspecting architect since that time. When was the building refurbished, by whom, and how were changes made? What effect did those changes have on the space and why were they made?

Find out the views of regular churchgoers. A questionnaire could be used or people could be interviewed; or have groups meet with all opinions being gathered.

'Do you like to worship with us all facing the front? Or do you like a circle or having people facing each other? What is it about worship and your sense of God that contributes to your liking this pattern?'

'Does the way we worship now help your sense of God? How?'

'Do you know stories of how our church developed this way? Do you know why the architect designed it this way (with a long nave and pews/in a square with huge pulpit)?'

'Why do you think changes have been made in the past, and how can those changes help us develop in our generation?'

'Are there issues about our building that worry you?'

It is helpful to every church to have a Mission Statement or a longer summary of what it wants to achieve and how it is setting out to achieve it. Many churches take their church council and longstanding members on an awayday to explore and state the elements of their mission.

A simplified example follows that summarizes one church's sense of mission and direction.

Purpose

Our purpose is to serve the people who live, work, visit or worship in Camden Town through the regeneration of St Michael's Church.

We will provide a sustainable future for St Michael's Church in its liturgical and pastoral ministry, in its service to its parish, and in the opening of the building to use by a wider public.

Aims

To provide a living place of worship and prayer in the middle of Camden Town.

To repair, restore and revitalize the church building.

To make the church open and accessible to all, and to provide community space in the Church Hall and in the new Parish Centre.

To develop arts programmes that celebrate and interpret the Christian tradition and heritage, the life of Camden Town or those who live in, work in or visit it.

To establish a financially viable future for the church.

We will work in partnership with other bodies (Borough and Government) to regenerate Camden Town, focusing particularly on job creation and community meeting space.

A workable format for a Mission Statement could start from biblical phrases that are then fitted to the unique location of the church and begin to inform the way worship and ministry take place.

'To love and worship God with our whole hearts, and minds and strength. We will engage in regular worship services and give financially to our church.'

'We will love our neighbours as ourselves. We will invite everyone who lives in St ____'s parish to join us in worship, share in our activities and enjoy fellowship together.'

'We will welcome and include the stranger who is in our midst. We will undertake a ministry of care for the poor, and support for refugees and asylum seekers.'

'We will seek to establish the kingdom of heaven in our parish. We will support initiatives for justice and peace and provide support to the best of our ability.'

Each church and parish will have its own unique set of priorities and interpretations of the Christian mission, but as soon as those injunctions become specific then the daily life of the church, the work of the members and the use of the building become implicated in mission.

Being open for fellowship outside of worship hours can welcome neighbours who are not Christian worshippers. Offering community service programmes on weekdays may bring relief to people in need, and provide an opportunity for strangers to meet together and become friends. And the building itself becomes the focus of activity and the common thread.

Being open every day has many practical implications. Are the facilities such as toilets available to visitors? Can the church run a small café to provide refreshment? Can the curious be welcomed with a guide that can enable them to know the church story of faith and what happens in the building during worship? Can the weary say a prayer, or rest their feet without interruption?

It is out of knowledge and understanding of the church and its members, and of the story of the building and the generations of faith, and by engagement with local residents and the needs of the area, that adaptations and changes to meet the present need will be integrated and find a form acceptable to people who have a stake in the building.

By exploring the values in relation to the building and mission that both those who are members and those who are outside have, we can find perspective on development, growth and change. The church mentioned above produced a set of values that undergird the way they intend to journey with their building. These values demand practical answers to questions about everything from staffing to facilities location and at the same time ensure that many aspects of concern are all taken into account.

Values

Worship

- We believe that every individual has a spiritual dimension and churches can make a place for their development.
- We will support additional uses which respect and relate to the building's Christian heritage.

Architecture and history

- We appreciate the inspirational qualities of the building's architectural heritage and believe they speak to the present day.
- We value the way in which the building's present condition commends it to those who visit and seek an appropriate approach to its restoration.

Community use

- We believe the building belongs to all who wish to use it.
- We recognize our responsibility as a church to provide a place of welcome and hospitality to people of other faiths and none.
- We believe Camden Town needs places which can contribute to the community development of the area.

Event use

- We believe the church can encourage and support the arts, cherish the story of the local community and enhance the quality of life and personal development of individuals.
- We believe in making the arts available to all, especially to provide an opportunity for those who do not have ready access to the arts.

Finance

- We believe that the combination of users in the church buildings should pay for its upkeep and maintenance.
- We welcome the opportunity to make financial contribution to the life of the local community.
- We recognize that we cannot fund the project alone.
- We believe that the church and the buildings will become sustainable financially.

Strategy for moving forward

It is common for churches facing a challenge with their buildings to feel overwhelmed with the pressures. Many clergy spend the majority of their time dealing with and worrying about building problems. At the same time they live with the stress of having increased loads of pastoral work with overall decreasing staff numbers in the church.

Set priorities with the Standing Committee or Building Committee.

Make a list of all the building issues, large and small, immediate or more long-term, without discriminating.

Now differentiate by coding each item:

- Long-term and Desirable (L&D).
- Long-term and Important (L&I).
- Regular and Important (R&I).
- Urgent but Minor (UbM).
- Urgent and Important (U&I).

To explain:

Long-term and Desirable. The redecoration of the church interior or aesthetic improvements that require major investment of time, energy or money are Long-term and Desirable. That is, they can wait, but you do want to get to them as soon as you can.

Long-term and Important. Refurbishing the church hall or creating new facilities in the church, so the building can begin to pay for itself and contribute productively to mission and ministry, are long-term and important. That is, they require significant investment of time, energy and resources to get under way but are critical to the overall sustainability of the church.

Regular and Important. These items are the building issues that recur but may take a long time to present themselves as a problem. They are essentially problems avoided by good housekeeping, and that includes many issues: gutter-cleaning, weed removal, lagging pipes that have a potential to freeze, and others you may identify.

Urgent but Minor. Every clergy person and most churchwardens receive a large number of trivial interruptions that have very little importance to the big picture. But in a church struggling to do more than merely survive, these issues can take over and consume all the available time.

Urgent and Important. Dealing with dangerous situations of falling stonework, trip hazards, and other health and safety issues require immediate attention or they very quickly become much bigger problems.

Once the list has been categorized set out a time plan.

Identify some time each week or month during which Urgent but Minor problems will be dealt with. For members of the church who regularly appear presenting these issues create a simple system such as a building items in-tray into which the member puts a note about these minor issues. At the designated time each month those who will clear up such issues (vicar and/or churchwardens, or volunteers) look through the items and work through the list, starting with those that seem most important. Those not completed are left for next month.

- Decide how the Urgent and Important items such as the Health and Safety Review will be undertaken (see p. 23), who will do it and when they will report back.
- For the Long-term and Important items such as creating facilities that will help fund the church, plan one or several meetings of the building committee when this will be the only item on the agenda. This will enable you to have full discussion and create a programme for achieving your goal. Allow no other items to impinge on this time by having an alternative method for dealing with minor crises, such as circulating notes, phone conversation or a small group with executive authority over minor items.
- For the Long-term and Desirable items set a date, maybe a year away, when these items will be next reviewed and addressed.

As each element of the church's building strategy evolves, continue to check that the facilities essential for mission are maintained, that underused space is allocated for productive, even income-generating, use and that buildings become the servant of mission.

Part 2

Managing Your Building

4

Health and Safety

Introduction

Every person and every organization is responsible for not causing harm to others by their own activity or behaviour. Even though churches are covered by insurance this will not protect them from legal retribution if someone is harmed by the church's negligence. The Health and Safety Executive is the government agency responsible for creating guidelines and for investigating problems. Unlike licensing, there is no officer who will visit your premises to check that good health and safety standards are being maintained, but if an accident or other incident happens then officers will investigate and take action.

Many guidelines produced for other organizations can be adapted to fit churches. Much information can be gleaned from the Internet to add to the summary below, which has been adapted from material from the Health and Safety Executive. Much of this long list of information is common sense, and many churches will have considered many aspects already.

Assessing the risks in your church

The Health and Safety Executive point out that a risk assessment on health and safety is 'a careful examination of what, in your work, could cause harm to people'. The focus is on identifying hazards that result in risk to ensure that action will be taken to reduce that risk to the minimum. The guidance is given as five key steps.[2]

---

2 From *Five Steps to Risk Assessment*, Health and Safety Executive leaflets, 1999.

Proceeding methodically through the key steps, taking brief notes as the steps are undertaken, can result in the basis of a health and safety document that is particular and appropriate to the individual church and a foundation for future review.

1 Look for the hazards.
2 Decide who may be harmed and how.
3 Evaluate the risks and decide whether the existing precautions are adequate or whether more should be done.
4 Record your findings.
5 Review your assessment and revise if necessary.

In every building there are features, equipment, materials and set-ups that could cause harm. Being very meticulous may result in a very long list. However, when you take the next step you may be able to note that many are already minimized.

Two or three people, preferably with different concerns in the life of the church, walk carefully through every area of the building to examine all the potential risks. Try to include someone who works closely with children, as their professional experience of children and hazards will be extremely helpful to a church that has or wants to include children in its life and mission. The Health and Safety Executive suggest ignoring the trivial items and concentrating on the more significant.

In every space and corner note down the potential hazards to health and safety. (If one of the churchwardens joins the walk around, it may also be helpful to take note of other items that are a hazard to security or good care of the building.) Look out especially for:

Potential items that could result in someone tripping or slipping: the uneven paving, uneven steps, items lying across corridors, slippery surfaces;

Occasional hazards such as doors that open into the pathway of someone unsuspecting;

Hazardous chemicals such as cleaning materials or corrosive materials;

Items stored badly, such as cleaning materials next to food and drinks ingredients;

For the security of the building ensure that old paint cans (even those with a useful drop left in them) are not stored anywhere in the building – they can add to the fire hazard.

Consider all gas and electricity supplies and equipment. Are all plugs and sockets checked regularly to ensure wiring has remained safe? Are there antiquated heaters in the vestry or parish room that ought to be checked by an electrician (all portable equipment should be checked from time to time and could go on the annual checklist of items the churchwardens address for their annual report)? Are floor-level power points in the Sunday School room and crèche covered by protective plug-ins when not in use, to protect inquisitive children? The major electrical and gas supply points should be subject to regular checks, but look out for overloaded plugs, too many adapters or potential overloading of sockets.

Many churches supplement their old and inadequate heating systems with Calor-gas-type heaters. These are an apparently simple portable solution. Have those that are in places where children may play or pass been protected by a fireguard? Are they protected from tipping over? Are all gas bottles taken out of the building when the building is not in use (they are a major and extremely dangerous hazard during any fire and are banned from many buildings)? Many insurance policies are invalidated if gas bottles are kept in the building (you may wish to read your policy small print or check with your insurance company or broker). Additionally, portable gas heaters produce a lot of water condensation which will cause damage to heritage churches.

If the church premises are to be used by children's groups the Children Act officer of the local council may ask for protection over very hot pipes and radiators.

Are all the doors that give access to areas that could be dangerous locked against improper entry? Are signs giving appropriate warning displayed where stairs, such as to the tower, are less than normal requirements, where treads are uneven or a handrail is not available?

Consider also the way spaces are used.

Children under eight years old should not have access to the kitchen and its equipment, and those over that age should not be in a working kitchen. Are there signs pointing this out to adults who use the kitchen?

Check the ways that church members are expected to handle items around the church. Are they encouraged to lift and carry things properly? Too often a shortage of volunteers results in people who are less than able struggling to achieve onerous tasks.

Does the church have its own ladders? Are these stored in a way that prevents misuse? Are those who use the ladders either taught to use them safely or well qualified to do so?

After making a list of all the items and the action to be taken, report fully to the church council.

Fire risks

Fire risks come not just from the passive causes that may be visible on a walk around the building but also from the way the building and its facilities are used.

What fire hazards are evident on the walkabout? Often the local fire brigade will visit to make a check on fire hazards and fire safety procedures, and that may be helpful in many cases. (However, your own check should include looking in storage areas for accumulations of material that might smoulder away undetected. Are rubbish bins emptied every time the building is vacated to ensure no paper bin might contain a lurking cigarette stub? You may ban smoking when your church is in use by various groups, but people will often still retire to the toilets to smoke, or drop a smouldering match into a kitchen rubbish bin.)

Keep doorways and corridors clear for access and emergency exit.

Electrical

Fire problems are often the result of poor maintenance and incorrect use. The guidelines may be fairly straightforward, but with many volunteers using church premises it is important to know who is responsible for the daily tasks and that the regular checks are in place. A sign-up sheet near the exit door with reminders of what must be done may be helpful.

Ensure that the regular checks on electrical supply and equipment are done.

Turn off all non-critical electrical appliances when everyone leaves.

Most churches have fire extinguishers in place, but have staff and volunteers been trained in how to use them? In a busy church an occasional fire drill may be useful. All staff should be trained also in the use of the different types of fire extinguishers.

Heating

While Calor gas or similar portable heaters with naked flames are easy to use, they are the most dangerous, because of both the naked flame in use and the presence of the bottles on the premises even when not in use.

For areas not reached by the main heating system, consider safer appliances: night storage, oil-filled or convector heaters.

Ensure that paper supplies or paper waste are away from heat sources, outlets or switching-points.

Smoking

Despite smoking not being a usual occurrence in church there are safeguards necessary, especially if the church or the hall is being used by various other organizations and groups. Display clear large No-Smoking signs. If necessary create a designated area. An outside porch can protect the determined smoker from the weather and discourage them from smoking in the toilets.

If smoking is allowed only outside, provide smoking bins just outside the door. Partially stubbed cigarettes in an internal bin that contains paper may burst into flame several hours later when no one is around to raise the alarm.

Fit a fire alarm system or, as a temporary measure, smoke alarms.

Candles have been the cause of many church fires – an overlooked candle around the Christmas tree, or candles and matches carelessly disposed of. Keep candles away from vestments and cloths, and extinguish all candles before leaving the building.

Waste that contains anything combustible should be removed from the building *every* day. Many churches store redundant equipment, materials and even jumble sale goods in nooks and crannies on balconies and various parts of the building. If it is essential to store such items, then fire safety should be addressed.

Arson

This happens to churches from time to time.

Store all combustible material or combustible liquids away from the building to reduce the arsonist's source of fuel. Lock away matches, candles and similar materials.

Policy

A written fire-safety policy is good strategy as all staff and volunteers can then be familiar with what they should do.

Include: keeping all fire exit routes and doors clear of debris and equipment, and unlocked whenever the building is in use.

Action to take on discovering a fire

Signs should explain how to raise the alarm and to whom; when the building is full for an event or service the rule may be different from when it is open to drop-in visitors.

Action to take on hearing the alarm

Give procedures for facilitating the exit by the congregation, the concert audience or activity group. Remember children's groups in the building may require more escorts and assistance. Parents may panic if in a different room from their children. For a busy church spend time training staff and volunteers in clearing people from the building and do so annually.

On a wall notice, indicate the location of the nearest phone, for calling the fire brigade.

Ensure that a plan of the building is available (off site) for the fire brigade.

Salvage and damage control

The church inventory should note items of value and how they may be most readily removed to a safe place in the case of fire. In your training sessions, note who will do this task while others clear people from the building. A list of high priority items (a grab list) may be kept offsite just in case.

Other risks around the building

Lone workers in the church are both very common and very vulnerable. Assess the potential dangers and danger areas and make plans to reduce the risk.

Can someone working in the (locked) office see into the church and who is approaching, ensuring they can keep themselves safe and phone for assistance?

The potential presence of money on the premises greatly increases the risk. Always remove money from the premises and make sure it is commonly known that this happens. Put up signs saying there is no money on the premises – it can act as a deterrent.

Distressed people seeking help in church do occasionally attack staff. Often this is because they have unrealistic expectations of how the church might or will help them. In churches with lone clergy the pressure can be extreme and training is needed for staff to realize how to both gently and firmly tell the person what limited help is available and address their own need for protection. Provide training for staff in how to take the pressure out of confrontations or difficult situations. At times it will be helpful to ensure that no one person is left to lock up the church alone and a panic alarm may be installed (ringing outside the church so that nearby businesses or residents may call for help).

Seek the advice of the diocese.

Hazardous substances

Church members often store hazardous materials in church in ways they never would at home. Cleaning materials should be locked away from any possibility of misuse or access by children. Under the sink in an unlocked cupboard is not adequate protection. Commercial cleaning materials are often stronger and more corrosive than those used domestically, and polishes and paints are flammable!

Office work space

Display screen equipment is required by law to be safe for employees and volunteers.

Ensure that all equipment and furniture is set at an appropriate height and reach for the worker. Shared desks can present problems: for example, an administrator working on a daily basis uses the unit set up for the vicar but doesn't like to 'complain'. Put up signs that enable staff both to check for signs of health problems related to their workspaces and to know how to adjust equipment. Ensure that work programmes include breaks away from the computer desk.

Maintenance and building work risks

Record any particular hazards that are present so these can be pointed out to anyone doing maintenance or repair work. This can include the presence of asbestos; do not leave knowledge of it to chance. Put caution signs on difficult access points.

Check that all ladders and other maintenance equipment are in excellent working order before anyone uses them. Check stepladders (and ensure users know how to lock this particular ladder in situ). Get rid of or repair wobbly or rickety ladders. Display safety posters, including one that shows how to use ladders at a correct angle to the ground.[3]

---

3 Available from building maintenance suppliers, or contact the Health and Safety Executive.

Safety of data

Apart from complying with data protection laws, remember to keep a backup of working files off the premises. Do a regular backup as often as every week.

Other safety instructions

Display important contact numbers ready for emergencies.

Ensure that water stopcocks, electrical trip switches and other such essential turn-off points are known by all staff or clearly signed.

When church staff are off the premises as part of their work, it is important to know where they are and when they plan to return. An emergency may require that they be contacted, or occasionally they may be in difficulty and knowing where they are may be critical to their safety. A simple system of a duplicate calendar on their desk with all current appointments entered, or a Post-it note on the desk, can tell others how to make contact.[4]

The Health and Safety Executive can be accessed on the web at www.hse.gov.uk/hse. See also: www.churchsafety.org.uk

Safety and the general public

With more and more churches open daily to visitors and open regularly for public events that are not worship there are a few key points to note.

Set out guidelines so that all vergers and volunteer staff know what is and is not permitted and how to deal with the many situations that arise. Train staff in basic skills including sorting situations out in non-confrontational ways. It is important to train staff not to have-a-go if a thief is spotted, and what to do if they or another person is attacked. It is more important to call for help than to become a second victim.

---

4 HSE Books, PO Box 1999, Sudbury, Suffolk, CO10 6FS, tel: 01787 881 165, supplies a wide range of booklets on safety and security for many office and public spaces, but as yet none specifically for churches.

Put up suitable signs (in the various languages of visitors) to reduce confusion and enable visitors to behave appropriately. For example, an unknowing visitor will not put their backpack on the communion table if it is roped off or a discreet sign says 'please do not place objects on the table'. Less 'policing' will be needed.

While not required by law, it can be extremely helpful to display safety signs, from EXIT to 'electric shock risk'. Such signs may be purchased[5] and some are 'glow-in-the-dark'. Since churches are or will be exempt from having a local authority licence for additional uses, many of the statutory requirements of places of entertainment, such as concert halls, are not compulsory. However, for those churches with a good programme of events a fair assessment should be taken on which of the requirements to adopt without the compulsion of law.

Keep a well-stocked first aid kit and an accident book[6] on the premises and a list of known first-aiders. When letting the church premises to other groups, it will be important for them to have access to the first aid kit and accident book, but they will have to provide their own first aiders.[7]

---

5 From HSE Books, as note 4.
6 A record of all accidents on the premises, entered on the day they happen. Accident Record Books can be purchased from major stationers.
7 Visit www.riddor.gov.uk/info to find more information on how the law applies to you.

5

Increasing Access

Access to the church is a current topic of interest with new Disability Access to public buildings becoming law in 2004.[8] However, improving access means many other things as well. Do potential visitors all have access to the physical plant, but also do potential visitors all have access to the programmes, services and activities that happen in the church? The issue is nearly as wide as equal opportunities for all.

At the centre of an access review are several key areas of investigation:

- A thorough examination of the physical environment to ensure that people with disabilities have open access.
- A thorough review of how the church operates to ensure that power, opportunity and responsibility are not restricted in a way that excludes certain people or groups.
- A careful review of timetables and staffing to ensure (especially for historic churches) that every possible opportunity is made for people to visit the church to appreciate the heritage.

The Heritage Lottery Fund booklet on improving access identifies several key areas of concern: the physical aspects, which are physical, sensory and intellectual access; then the organizational, social, cultural and financial issues that are less visible but equally powerful.

How to start an access review:

1 Consult present users of the building to identify any discouraging features.
2 Ask people in the neighbourhood (volunteers with clipboards outside the local shops, for example) how easy they find access to the

---

8 See under 'Access plans' in the Resources section.

church and whether anything discourages them, factors that might, can or cannot be changed.

3 With the inspecting architect if necessary, undertake a detailed exploration of the physical aspects of the building, recording the process with notes on a floorplan and other drawings, if possible accompanying this with photographs of key items.

In a review meeting consider the following questions raised by the Heritage Lottery Fund.

Organizational barriers may include: the image presented, the opening hours (or lack of them), the type of information provided, limits put in the way of enjoying the space. Staff may inadvertently discourage visitors by their manner, and some training about the needs of visitors may be helpful. Or consider new signage. For example, the verger may be fed up with people asking to use the toilet and where it is. That 'fed up'-ness will communicate as grumpiness with the visitor. Consider toilet signage and work together on the manner of dealing with the needs of visitors.

Similarly, it may be very obvious to people in the church how the building is used, how the various key features function in the life of the church. But is it obvious to visitors? Can they understand the living church from the material which is presented on the bookstall or entry table? It is common for churches to have a history booklet. But does the church have an illustrated booklet explaining the font and its use, the pulpit, the communion table, the choir stalls and clergy desks as they function in worship? To this could be added the use of the church as a place for weddings and funerals and how to make arrangements. None of this is as obvious to outsiders or even local residents as it is to regular churchgoers. In particular, consider what explanations are offered to children: are they effectively excluded by the intellectual barrier of everything being presented in concepts and language that is beyond their grasp?

Physical barriers may be in the path of people with limited mobility, in wheelchairs, the old or people with children in buggies. Consider steps and stairs, narrow passageways, steep pathways, gates that are difficult to manoeuvre, floor and other ground surfaces. English Heritage's guidelines ask first whether access can be provided without alterations to the building. This can involve relocating a public function to the ground floor rather than the first, adjusting the circulation route, making alternative presentation of materials. Any planned alteration to the building must consider its heritage value and the sensitivity of particular features, and sufficient emphasis being made on an entrance that is accessible. The diocesan or local authority conservation officer may be able to offer expert advice on the solutions to physical barriers in listed churches.

Before taking action to change the building physically, double check that the proposed change will really meet the need. Ensure the alterations conform to best practice in conservation.

For very detailed consideration of physical features, including the church office, the Church House publication *Widening the Eye of the Needle* is extremely useful.

Sensory barriers may stand in the way of people with hearing or sight limitations. Many churches now have an induction loop. Some have signs in Braille. Many are adopting large-print service sheets and notices. For visitors, can an audiocassette be provided? Can those supervising or helping visitors be trained more fully?

Social and cultural barriers. Many urban churches today find themselves located in a changing residential and business environment with many people of different languages and faiths around them. Has provision been made for information both written and oral for people for whom the church may be a strange place? Having an open day that describes and explains the church and its use in languages and concepts that are accessible to new local residents can be effective. Consider offering refreshments that are culturally familiar to the visitors even more than to the hosts.

Visits by local schoolchildren will include those from other faith groups and religious experience. Start thinking from their viewpoint, language and concepts in preparing material that can help them appreciate and understand the church, its functions and its history.

6

Maintenance

Certain responsibilities for the care of church buildings are delegated to the churchwardens, and it is their task to see, in co-operation with the minister, that these are appropriately delivered. Very often churchwardens are people with no experience of caring for buildings and especially not major public buildings that are listed. Sometimes a congregation has someone with more knowledge and skills to whom they can turn. Use this as an opportunity to learn, not to hand the responsibility on. For some tasks the advice of the church's inspecting architect (responsible for the five-yearly Quinquennial Inspection and Report) will be invaluable.

Several tasks are legal requirements:

- *To compile a full record of all the property belonging to the church – called a terrier – and an inventory of all the articles that belong to the church.* Churches often own smaller items not used in church that, for example, may be in another place for safekeeping, and these too should be listed. Consider, church paintings and photos in the Parish Room or the Vicarage, vestments on display, silver pieces at the bank. For items in the church and the church safe it is advisable to have a photographic record and then, should the worst case happen and burglary or fire takes place, there is a record that is usable both by police and by the insurance company.
- *To maintain a record of all work done to the church – a logbook – with relevant papers and related financial information.* When building works are undertaken the architect and the builder will produce detailed drawings of the structure, and an engineer will supply detailed information on the way everything electrical and mechanical is fitted. Keep all this information filed together and accessible as, sometime in the future, the layout of the drains or the route of wiring systems will be needed again. During building works it is now required by law that a safety supervisor

is employed to check every aspect of safety during works and to give the client a safety report about the use of the building and its facilities when it is handed over. Not only should this report be filed for future availability but at least some members of the church council should be familiar with its contents. It is an essential tool for the health and safety of those who use the church (see health and safety policy, p. 23). Such an annual review may also include a review of insurance with the insurance company representative, as changes in use may require that the church insurance be upgraded or up-rated.

- *To send a copy of the inventory to the diocesan officer to whom the archdeacon asks for it to be sent.* For many aspects of running a church the diocese has a responsibility for oversight, in this case for buildings but also for ensuring that church finances comply with Charity Law. When a new incumbent arrives in a church it is often a good time to check that all such information is up to date and copies have been sent to the appropriate people.
- *To inspect the church building at least annually.* An outline for a maintenance plan is given on pp. 38–41. It is advisable for the churchwardens and the minister and any other key person to walk around to check that everything has indeed been done appropriately. They are advised also to check that records of cyclical checks on such things as fire extinguishers, lift maintenance, lightning conductor, electrical safety checks, are all recorded as complete in the past year. The inspections should be a physical walk around and into as many accessible spaces as possible, checking for any visible problems in the building.
- *To make an annual report to the church council at the meeting next before the annual general meeting.*
- *To make the same (or revised if the church council suggested) report to the church's annual general meeting on behalf of the church council.*
- *Each year for the churchwardens to bring the up-to-date terrier and logbook to a church council meeting together with all the relevant records of what has been done.* The reason is that the role of the churchwardens in regard to the building is executive, that is, they do their work on behalf of the church council. They should produce a signed form that states that all the records are accurate and up to date. It would helpful to do this around the time of their annual inspection of the building so the church council can be made aware of any concerns that arise from the inspection. Because of their particular role in regard to the building the churchwardens may also be the best people on the church council to keep the Quinquennial Inspection Report in perspective, pointing out target dates for completing work.

- *To comply with any order by the archdeacon to remove items to a place of safety*. There are times in the life of a church building when the church's precious or vulnerable possessions are unsafe in the building. The reason may be potential ingress of water that may cause damage; it may be that security is inadequate for items of that value; it may be that items such as precious vestments must be repaired and should not be handled until repaired; or it may be that present use such as activity sessions could result in damage to vulnerable items. Sometimes the archdeacon (or even the Diocesan Advisory Committee) may require that items not be removed even temporarily as in past experience such items have been lost, dropped from terriers and disposed of from the place of storage.

It is the responsibility of the church council, usually exercised through the churchwardens, to ensure that a number of key building care tasks are regularly undertaken. The church council should be in the picture as many of the tasks on larger churches can only be undertaken by appropriately skilled people, and the church council will need to pay for this work.

The sad tale with many churches is that in a climate of financial pressure such work as is listed below is ignored or considered not pressing enough for money to be allocated. But many churches do find themselves facing major financial pressure when a gutter blocked for several years has resulted in an ongoing trickle of water into the church or walls or roof timbers and has caused many thousands of pounds worth of damage. 'Look after the pennies and the pounds will look after themselves', and many other such sayings, are applicable. At the annual budget-setting meeting of the church council a well prepared report from the churchwardens will advise the council when and how much will need to be spent on the building over the next year on all protective maintenance work.

- Regularly inspect the gutters, preferably when it is raining. Look both outside and inside the church. Look for places where a sagging gutter is pouring water down the walls rather than carrying it along to the hopper heads and downpipes. Look at the hopper heads in heavy rain: are they adequate for getting all the water away in the downpipes or are they overflowing and damaging brick and stonework? A blocked downpipe will also result in an overflowing hopper head. Churches with parapet gutters often have blocked drains not visible at all from the ground, and these must be inspected from above; all sorts of items from falling leaves to tennis balls or dead pigeons may keep these essential points from functioning well, and the water simply backs up and flows into the buildings. It may be helpful in any case to have a word with inspecting architects about the adequacy of gutters and drains as recent climate change has resulted in less frequent but far heavier rainstorms for which old water disposal systems were not designed. Check that water is flowing away from all surface drains effectively and that they have not gradually filled up with the dust that has been washed from pavements and gardens.

- Whenever it snows get used to having a look at trouble points. Ice may gather in hopper heads and melting snow may then flow into the building or down the walls. Discuss with the inspecting architect improvements in access to critical areas that are vulnerable in poor weather.

Spring or early summer

- Make the annual inspection and prepare the report for the church council, checking the inventory and updating the logbook.
- Check that bird-proofing mesh is in place and effective. Consider with the architect any solutions for continuing problems. Birds can cause significant problems to health and safety as well as their detritus being unsightly.
- Sweep out high-level places that have accumulated rubbish such as falling leaves. If there are bats in the church their presence should be reported to English Nature and they should be left undisturbed. Sadly or gladly, the church is required to look after them.
- Ivy (and any other plants) growing on the building cause significant damage even while temporarily looking picturesque. The roots will creep into the surface of stone, brick or mortar and break it up. Once that hard surface of the building material is cracked the wind, rain and frost quickly begin to erode the surface. Use a weedkiller on ivy to prevent it re-establishing itself. Many church walls have a layer of cement at the foot, giving a hard surface encouraging water to fall away from the building. Discourage all plant growth here, especially in the cracks, as water will soon find its way into the walls and rise inside. Spray with weedkiller.
- Check the heating installation; get the boiler professionally serviced and flues cleaned. Then there will be no panic in the autumn when it is time to switch on again.
- Beetles in timbers are most obvious between mid-April and mid-June

when they will leave obvious areas of dust and other residue. At their most serious, such infestations will cause huge amounts of damage and untold cost of replacement.

- Look out also for any areas of damp that suggest that water is sitting there rather than being carried away. There may be changes in plaster colour, flaking paint, discoloured brick or even fungi as evidence of water damage. Get immediate advice from the inspecting architect to prevent further ingress and make plans for repair before the problems spreads. Rot grows like fungus once water has weakened the structure of the building material concerned.
- Wherever there are ventilators, check these are cleaned out and functioning well.

Summer

- Keep the grass cut. Growth of weeds and grass close to the church walls can also hide problems that should be addressed, especially keeping water standing around the base of the walls.
- Check again on ivy and other intrusive weeds. Any church with buddleia growing in its walls and gutters has a serious problem, even though the butterflies may find it attractive. The root system will both block the gutter and send water into the building and eat into the wall materials and enable weather damage to increase.
- Summer is the best time for external painting to railings, window frames and elsewhere. Regular painting decreases the chance of rust in the ironwork or rot in wooden frames. Another stitch in time.

Autumn

- As autumn approaches the weather is going to be increasingly threatening, so it's time to check that all gutter and water disposal is in good order. Churches with trees anywhere nearby may have to have gutters cleaned two or more times each year, but autumn is clearly the most critical time.
- As often as once each year it is worth having all surface drains rodded through or jetted out as accumulations of soil or rubbish brought down by heavy rain may cause water to back up into the building. Clear all drains right through to where they join the public system in the roadway,

including under the pavements. The local authority is responsible for drains beyond this point, but not for anything on the church's land.

- Rubbish should be cleared from all ventilation points inside and outside and broken covers repaired. As the weather gets colder all kinds of vermin will use them as access into the building. As the autumn progresses into winter look out for signs that vermin have found their way in and deal with them as soon as possible to limit the damage.
- During spells of freezing weather, look out for the related problems of burst pipes or blocked drainage.
- Check radiators and 'bleed' them as necessary to keep the heating system working at its best.

Annually

- All fire extinguishers must be serviced annually and will normally have a log attached to them that indicates the most recent service date. The company that services them will, if asked, check that sufficient extinguishers of the relevant types are located in the building. Remember to check that extinguishers are on appropriate wall fittings and are not shifted to be used as doorstops. Having extinguishers is only useful if someone knows how to use them. Arrange that key people, churchwardens, servers, ministers are trained in how to use fire extinguishers and which extinguisher to use in what circumstance. Repeat the training from time to time – it is easy to forget unfamiliar information in an emergency.
- In bad weather, steps and other points of access should be checked to ensure that access has not become hazardous (more aspects of this are covered in the section on health and safety). Keep a bucket of sand or fine gravel for sprinkling on icy steps and pathways. Ensure there is adequate lighting for people attending meetings or services on dark evenings so that they can see steps and other hazards that might cause problems.

Every five years the electrical system should be checked for safety by a suitably qualified electrician. The lightning conductor should also be checked.

Similarly, external ironwork, window frames, and woodwork such as fascia boards will require repainting. This may be as often as every three years. Ask for the inspecting architect's advice.

Some churches may require special attention to heating levels because of fixtures and fittings as well as for care of the congregation. If the church has significant murals or paintings these may be damaged by fluctuations in temperature. The inspecting architect or a specialist conservator will be glad to advise. Similarly vestments and other cloth articles should be protected from damp that often accumulates if ventilation is inadequate.

The Ulster Historic Churches Trust produces a *Maintenance Schedule for Churches and Good Housekeeping Guide* that includes a 'Diary' for all the tasks of church care and maintenance. It helpfully adds a page for the necessary signatures at annual report time, but more particularly has a grid for recording essential contact information for key people. This would be incredibly helpful, not just for maintenance but also for emergencies. The list suggests recording details of names, addresses and phone numbers for the local police and fire brigade; insurance company, with relevant policy numbers; alarm company, with passwords and policy numbers; fire safety equipment company, with contract number; builder, plumber, electrician, heating engineer, architect and key holders.

Resources

From Church House Publishing:

> *The Churchwarden's Year: a Calendar of Church Maintenance*
> *Church Log Book*
> *Church Property Register* (Terrier and Inventory)
> *The Care of Church Plate* (and many other small booklets on aspects of caring for church fabric and contents)
> *A Guide to Church Inspection and Repair*

How to Look After Your Church, Council for the Care of Churches, Church Information Office, 1970–.

The Joint Repair Scheme of English Heritage and the Heritage Lottery Fund produces an outline for a schedule of planned maintenance.

And see Church Care www.churchcare.co.uk

7

Repair

Every Church of England church – and each main denomination has its own requirements – is required to undergo an inspection every five years, called the Quinquennial Inspection. The legislation (since 1991) requires every *diocese* to make provision, and the inspection is normally commissioned and paid for by the diocesan administration.

The scope of the inspection includes not just the structure of the building and its integrity but also any items that are architecturally, artistically, historically or archaeologically significant or of significant financial value. This covers items that are movable as well as those that are fixed.

After a day or so of inspection, climbing up to roofs, scanning spires with binoculars and examining wood for signs of decay, or even cracks for signs of recent movement, the architect will prepare a comprehensive summary of their observations. These will be accompanied by a set of recommendations prioritizing the work over the next five years; for example, a Category A list that must be done urgently, within 2 years; a Category B for 2 to 5 years, and then any remaining items that should be tackled before the next inspection. In addition to these specific recommendations, expect the architect to note such things as the expected life span of the existing roof covering or other key areas of the building. For churches with older systems there may be similar observations about heating, electrical and drainage systems that on a regular cycle need replacing. Such observations will enable those who oversee the care of the church building to create a plan, maybe as long as ten years, showing what works will be needed and as far as possible the projected cost.

To prepare for the visit of an inspecting architect who will be making the report, it is advisable that someone is on site if the access points are locked or it is not easy to leave a set of keys and let the architect find everything for themselves. Expect the architect to need access to tower, crypt, boiler room, vestries and any other spaces that may normally be locked. Similarly if the church owns ladders that give access to gutters, parapets and roofs, these should be made available. If the church has no such equipment, expect the architect to arrange for a local builder to be on site with ladders and to pass on the cost of the builder's attendance on site to the diocese.

The architect will also need to see the church inventory (a book listing all the church's items of property) and the logbook of all the work that has been undertaken on the building. This will enable the architect to comment on works that have been done in the past five years.

The Quinquennial Inspection report is sent to the church council, the vicar or minister, the archdeacon (or equivalent) and the secretary of the Diocesan Advisory Committee. The latter two recipients do nothing with the report other than note its contents! The church and its vicar are responsible for taking action. The church council members should be advised of the contents of the report but its best use is in the development of a plan for work on the building.

While most architects will be happy to include some consideration of the costs involved in the remedial works advised in the quinquennial report, further work must be done before these figures can be considered the *real* cost of suggested work. For all but very small items of work the full budget for the work should be established. That is, the cost of the building works at current prices, the fees for architect and other professional advisers and Value Added Tax. For all but the smallest projects these prices are best set by a quantity surveyor who will not be taking the projected figure from a recently completed fairly similar piece of work, but from current prices in the building industry and will add in a suitable contingency figure and mark-up to cover any delay in the works that can be anticipated while the church raises the necessary funds.

The professional adviser

From this Quinquennial Inspection system we get the practice of each church having an inspecting architect, a professional with appropriate architectural skills taken from a list of people of whom the Diocesan Advisory Committee approves. For example, the list ensures that a person with appropriate conservation expertise looks after a Grade I listed medieval church rather than an architect with experience in modern housing or retail space.

In practice, most inspecting architects are appointed by agreement between Diocesan Advisory Committees and the local church. Often with a change of incumbent or with a major project being undertaken a church may begin to think a new architect is needed. Taking into account that the Diocesan Advisory Committee's chief role will be protective, the architects recommended may well be more experienced in conservation than in working on new buildings.

It is possible to appoint a different architect for a specific project, such as creating church hall provision, if the church believes this second architect has more relevant experience. It will be important to have a competitive tender process when preparing for new work and a new contract with each professional adviser. This will enable the church to compare the skills and experience of several architects (even if you already have a good idea of which one you want) as well as comparing the scales of fees that the various architects will charge. For more detail on appointing an architect, see below at p. 46.

Most inspecting architects are experienced at working with church councils to address the necessary building repair works. Once the church council has received the report it is advisable to meet together with the architect and work out whether, for example, there is any work that can be undertaken by volunteers. Often the quality of work required and the processes that must be followed cannot be assured with voluntary labour.

The architect may advise that there is particular work for which a specialist report is needed. Some church roofs and spires are so inaccessible that abseilers may be commissioned to check out in detail what high-level work is needed, or stained glass may require a specialist to consider its repair. Historic woodwork or murals may need a conservation plan from a specialist conservator before action can be taken to clean or repair such items. A new heating or electrical system may require detailed consideration by a specialist who can evaluate the various possible options and recommend the best kind of system for the future. Getting the right specialist advice is never a waste of time.

Changing architects

From time to time, churches decide they would like a different architect. It may be that with a new vicar the pace of change picks up, and new works are required for which the church would like to see new design ideas, or it may be that with their own architect retiring the alternative suggested by the practice is not someone with whom the church is comfortable.

First, what does the church want the architect to do? Is it time to deal with repairs highlighted by the Quinquennial Inspection report, reordering, or a new development? Will the new architect replace the existing architect or work with them? Ask the diocese for information of churches that have faced similar issues and find out who helped them and how good the solution was.

Then, create a shortlist of potential architects. The Diocesan Advisory Committee secretary may have some suggestions. The church members may have suggestions, though the Quinquennial Inspection architect will have to be on the diocese's accepted architects list. In looking for potential candidates there are several criteria that should help create a good shortlist:

- For a listed building, architects with experience in conservation architecture and repair of historic buildings. Churches do find themselves struggling to make new repairs to badly designed work of the past.
- For new building works or alterations to the church, architects with experience of church and public buildings and design skills, so they understand the needs of liturgy, pastoral work, circulation of people in multi-use space, security.
- Where there are both kinds of work the architect should be able to offer examples of both kinds of work and how they met the clients' needs in the designs.
- Choose a selection panel from among the church council members and arrange an interview process.
- Select the vicar and churchwardens, as they will have a key role in communication with the architect on behalf of the church. Select one or two additional people who may have particular roles or experience with building works or building issues.
- Write to each of the architects the church wishes to interview, introducing the church and outlining the work that is anticipated in the near

future. If this is the interview for a particular architectural project, outline that project.

- Allow time for the architects to visit the church before the interview, so allow a month or more. Ask the architects to explain their own approach to the building and tell of similar projects they have tackled and the outcomes.
- It is easiest to have the interviews all one half-day or day, so that the interview panel remains the same, and information about each architect is not forgotten by the time the decision is made.
- A good process is to allocate each architect 30 minutes for the interview and leave 15 minutes between interviews for the panel to complete notes and if necessary get refreshments.
- Take notes as the interviews are in progress, about how the architect responds to key concerns of the panel.
- It is preferable to make the decision just after the last interview is over, not to leave it to another day when other impressions will have intervened. (For more information on interviewing see pp. 137–8.)
- If the interview is not for appointing the quinquennial or inspecting architect, but about a specific project, then it is appropriate to ask the architect about their fee level. It is adequate if they say for example that they charge on the scale recommended by the Royal Institute of British Architects, as this gives you assurance that the charges will be calculated appropriately. RIBA fee calculations are on a sliding scale, with a lower percentage being charged on higher cost work and higher percentages being charged on smaller projects or highly technical or intricate work. Replacing a roof is a large but not intricate project if it involves replacing the slates that are all alike. Repairing stone tracery or similar conservation work is intricate and more time-consuming for the architect.

If the process has been well prepared then it is likely that several of the architects could equally achieve the work to the necessary standard and in this case the panel can choose the architect with whom they believe they can work most effectively.

The decision of the panel may need to be ratified by the church council, but since they were not party to the interviews they cannot appropriately change from the recommended candidate.

When writing to the successful candidate also remember to write with thanks for their time to those who were unsuccessful on this occasion.

Conservation

'Conservation' is the contemporary term used in the heritage sector for work on listed buildings rather than 'restoration'. 'Restoration' implies work that will make the building as it was when it was first built or installed. The latter is rarely possible or even acceptable. 'Conservation' describes working with an old item without making it look new but at the same time stopping deterioration and repairing any accumulated damage. Over the years wood darkens, for example, and it is not possible to return to the pristine condition, but it is possible to remove faded and cracked varnish and replace it with something new and non-invasive. The conservator may recommend removing Victorian paint from Georgian panelling and refinishing in another more appropriate way, but ultimately restoration to its pristine state is neither achievable or desirable.

For listed churches it is extremely helpful to have a conservation plan prepared by the church's architect and other specialists; this is especially true for large or particularly important churches. For example, many churches have a conservation plan for their organ and for unique historic features; it can be advisable to have other such reports for windows, carving, furniture and fittings; but the conservation plan will consider the church's structure itself.

The report includes historical material as well as outlining best practice in conservation and recommendations which will become agreed policies for the particular features and elements of the building.

There is a cost involved for the professional work, but the conservation plan gives a good perspective when decisions are to be made about repairs or on the cycle of maintenance and renewal.

The conservation plan will give the overall history of the building, its architecture and how it has been used. A building cannot be understood and appreciated by just looking at its physical features; the story of its use and its development as a place of worship all inform the plan. For example, a listed church may have pews. The church may be 400 years old but the pews are Victorian. The conservation plan will outline the story that resulted in the pews being installed, their relative historical value, their state of repair and any factors that would inform decisions about their future, such as how best to maintain and repair them, how to polish or not polish and if questions were to be raised about removing them, give information that would help inform that decision.

Such a plan helps inform the church council with a sense of responsibility and stewardship for their building. Congregations may be interested in elements of the reports, as all too often individuals are unaware of the value or uniqueness of the familiar environment. In particular, those who clean and care for the building would be appalled if by doing something obvious they were causing damage. Again an example: the regular washing of a Victorian tiled floor eventually caused the tiles to bow up from the surface beneath, like a shallow bubble; the reason was that the tiles were gradually absorbing the water (they are dry clay after all) and expanding, thus no longer fitting together.

New works or major alterations

New work in a church or heritage building has to take into account the existing, including the history of the architecture and worship and ministry.

The English Heritage booklet *New Work in Historic Places of Worship* raises issues and ideas that will help a church with the essential preliminaries in preparing for new work. Always start with a statement of significance and a statement of need as this will ground the development in the context of the overall impact on the building.

A story from such a church may help. This church was preparing to rebuild its hall, and instead of leaving the hall some twenty yards from the church, wanted to build the new hall adjoining the church so that facilities could be shared and would add to the access of churchgoers to ancillary facilities such as the kitchen and disabled-accessible toilet. The new first draft plan suggested that the only location for the hall was adjoining the west wall with a new entrance into the church from the foyer that was common with the hall and its facilities. Could a doorway be made through the wall? Additionally the font was located close to the west wall and effectively in the way of those who would enter the new door. To where could it be moved?

These questions are not just about heritage issues, the age of the wall or the font or their materials. There are additional considerations. The font is located near the entrance to the church so that the location of key features, the presentation of the word, the communion table and the font are symbolic of the journey. The Christian enters the Church of God through baptism and then journeys to the presence of God in receiving communion. The liturgy of baptism in the contemporary Church is most often celebrated in the context of the parish communion, symbolizing that the baptized person is being welcomed as Christian and as member of this specific church not just the Church generally; therefore it is important for the congregation to see the baptism or be able to gather with the family around the font. In our particular case, to move the font forward a few feet would maintain the image of journey but be so close to pews that few people could gather around it and even fewer see the event. There was much ongoing discussion.

Sometimes new extensions to churches are designed as if the original architect has planned them, imitating materials and roof angles, doorways and windows, but more often a new and innovative design gets approval. In the latter case design work should include quality of materials, perspectives and facilities that are worthy of being alongside a listed building. With new extensions on ancient buildings, an important consideration will be the view of the building. Do not plan to block the view of it from its main approaches; instead locate the extension, if possible, where the view is not an issue.

Internal reordering is a significant issue. Again an architect who understands both heritage buildings and the needs of the contemporary Church will be most able to create an acceptable design. Spend a lot of time preparing the brief (see p. 100) so the architect is responding to specific needs and can advise on the most acceptable way to meet these needs in this specific context in a way that is acceptable to the various authorities who will need to give permission. Don't get into the trap of 'designing' the solution as a means of expressing the need when you prepare the brief for the architect. If you ask the architect to design a toilet in the seldom-used south porch, they will do so, but it may not be the best place to locate a toilet in your church. Tell the architect what toilet facilities are needed, how often they will used (for example, occasionally on Sunday morning and during intervals at monthly concerts) and ask the architect to respond from their expertise.

New faith and new mission

Sometimes new clergy arrive with new ideas, new sense of mission and lots of ideas for change. An ancient building cannot always adapt easily. New mission starts with new faith and commitment and not with a change to the building. Removing all the pews will not bring new people into the church, but a vibrant Christian congregation will. Allow new energy and vitality for mission first to find its identity as a church, only then consider how the building might adapt to meet the actual need. In the past few decades many churches have adopted revised seating arrangements and relocated the communion table in locations that are strangely at odds with the lines and orientation of their buildings, all in the name of becoming flexible. Within a year or two the arrangement has become as fixed and inflexible as the old pews!

However, as congregations grow – and many do – there are needs for additional seating, sight of screens for projected song words, for more fellowship facilities, or a greater ability to move around. A good architect will respond to these in the context of the church's conservation plan, that is, a good sense of its ongoing history as well as its present need.

8

Faculty Jurisdiction and the Diocesan Advisory Committee

No repair or alteration maybe made to a Church of England church without Faculty permission. That is permission through the legal processes of the church hierarchy that results in a 'faculty' being approved by the diocesan chancellor. Some small and urgent repairs may be approved by an archdeacon, but this is not the norm. The chancellor's decision is informed primarily by the Diocesan Advisory Committee, who will have reviewed all the necessary information about the planned works. This committee usually includes not just the archdeacons but also a cross-section of professional advisers in everything from archaeology to glass conservation.

A simple rule of thumb can be applied to building works on churches. If the building is not broken do nothing to it; if it is broken fix it with like materials; and if something new is planned make it strikingly new (often but not quite always) and of a quality that fits with the existing building.

The faculty process is fairly straightforward, but although in some dioceses it is done more quickly and efficiently than others, it is still lengthy.

Talk to the archdeacon about the planned work. Since the archdeacon will in most cases be at the Diocesan Advisory Committee meetings, it is best to explain why the work is needed, how the particular solution to a problem has been arrived at and precisely what work is planned. The archdeacon's comments will not be just a personal view but considered advice on how best to make progress with the work.

Explain your plan to the Secretary of the Diocesan Advisory Committee before the formal submission of a request. Again it is advisable to include well-prepared notes on how the need for work has arisen, what the church's professional advisers are recommending and the work the church is planning. The Secretary will also advise on the best time to consult outside bodies with an interest such as English Heritage, Council for the Care of Churches, and amenity societies such as the Victorian or Georgian Societies.

Once the Diocesan Advisory Committee is sent the formal application (from the church council led by the church's architect if it is for building works; by the church council if it is for a change that does not involve building works, such as a change of use to meet a pastoral need) the Secretary may recommend a preliminary visit by some specialists from the committee to look at the plans *in situ*. This advance group are then able make an informed presentation to the committee when it meets. The Diocesan Advisory Committee may want to know the views of a variety of consultees before proceeding. In some dioceses the applicant church and its professionals are invited to make a presentation when the case is considered by the committee. In other dioceses, there is no representation and archdeacons are the key persons making the case for the local church. This makes the preliminary conversation with the church's archdeacon particularly important.

The Diocesan Advisory Committee may advise against the works, make suggestions for change to the planned works or may simply recommend them. The next step is to apply to the chancellor (again the application is from the church council, and the architect is the lead person) for formal approval with the supporting statement from the Diocesan Advisory Committee. In the case of historic churches the chancellor may seek advice from other interested bodies such as English Heritage, Council for the Care of Churches, the Victorian Society or the Georgian Society during a consideration stage. The church will, upon application for faculty, be sent a small notice that has to be displayed outside the building so that members of the public may respond or object to the proposed works. Sometimes an objector will remove the objection when they realize the necessity for the work, or if their point is spurious the chancellor can ignore it. The Diocesan Advisory Committee secretary or the archdeacon will advise on how to deal with objectors. Then when the public notice period has been completed and all paperwork is in place the chancellor makes a decision. If the church has carefully made its case and consulted interested outsiders during its own planning phase, even fairly dramatic changes can gain approval.

However, if the chancellor considers the work inappropriate it cannot go ahead. The appeal process is lengthy, costly and likely to be unsuccessful. It is advisable rather to listen carefully to all the reasons that faculty has not been granted and ask the church's professional adviser to seek an alternative way to achieve the church's aims.

For pastoral changes, rather than building works, the archdeacon or equivalent is the best first point of contact in getting permission to make changes.

Historic churches that are listed buildings

Churches of the six major denominations are currently exempt from the usual local authority listed building consent process because that process is devolved to the denominational system of faculty jurisdiction. However, if work is planned on the outside of a listed church, whether repair or alteration, planning permission may also be required from the local authority. The church architect will advise the church on this and make the applications on their behalf. All works whether under faculty jurisdiction or not will come under the requirements of Building Regulations and will require visits from the local authority building regulations officers to approve the work. Their concern is mostly to do with issues such as safety both during and after works are done.

If the alterations to a church involve a change of use, the church will also need planning permission from the local authority, that is if the church wishes to change from or add a function that is not essentially about being a church, for example, running a café on weekdays.

Archdeacons, Diocesan Advisory Committees and architects know a great deal about consents procedures and who has to be consulted and when. If in any doubt ask for information early on in the programme while you are still at the ideas stage with your architect so that any barriers to progress can be dealt with constructively before expensive drawing-up of plans has happened.

Resources

A Guide for the Quinquennial Inspection of Churches, Diocese of Birmingham, 1993.

See www.churchcare.co.uk for information on statements of significance and of need.

9

Change of Use and Additional Uses

Change or additional uses in a church building require a great deal of preparation. What are the reasons for change? What are the best changes to meet the needs of the church in its worship and ministry? What options were considered before choosing these particular changes? Can the congregation afford to run the building once changes are made? Who is going to pay for the construction programme? Will the change impact negatively on a fine heritage building?

Preparation

Prepare a statement of significance and a statement of need – based on a comprehensive understanding of the building, its history and its use, its neighbourhood, its demographics and the building's physical context. What contemporary need results in the need for change in use, and how does that change best fit into the significance and context? (See pp. 95–9 for more about preparatory stages.) Bear in mind that each of these factors is of compelling if not equal importance and must be understood and responded to as change is planned.

Evidence of need for change?

Using maps of the catchment and potential catchment area of the building, identify on the map:

- Community centres.
- Health centres, hospitals and schools.

- Shops and industrial places.
- Residential areas and kinds of housing.

Mark in the walking routes that people use to get to public transport, take children to school or go shopping. These may indicate more people who, given the right facilities and programmes, might be interested in the church and its programmes. Many people who pass a church that is closed on weekdays assume it is no longer used and of no interest. Becoming an openly 'everyday' church can drastically alter local perception.

Using demographic information from local sources (borough, health authority or other sources), identify target needs that may not be met fully already in the area. For example, space for social events, childcare, youth programmes, work with the elderly, exercise and fitness, refugees and homeless.

Collect together records of enquiries about space to let, space for performance and other uses as evidence of need. Encourage enquirers to send letters stating their need and interest.

Meet with officers of the local council, especially social services and community development. Contact the area health authority about community health initiatives for which space is needed. Talk to the local Council for the Voluntary Sector, as they will have contact with many community organizations and charities that may be seeking space.

As the particular level of interest becomes apparent, only then begin to form a strategy for future use. Some of the groups who are first and fastest at wanting to get your commitment to their use of your space may be counterproductive; they may be moving because of financial problems they had elsewhere (take up references) or difficult to combine with other uses for health and safety reasons (like the dog club). Wait until a fuller picture of potential uses forms before making decisions.

Faculty

Any change of use in church facilities (as well as any modification or repair to the building or its contents) requires faculty permission. The process for getting faculty permission is explained on p. 110. If in doubt talk to the archdeacon or the secretary to the Diocesan Advisory Committee.

Staff time and resources for new uses

Assess the resources the church has or will need for extended uses of its building or buildings. If the clergy are to continue to serve the pastoral and liturgical needs of the parish then who will do the additional work that being open every day involves? There are still country village churches that are open daily with no one 'on duty', but more urban environments need the security of someone being present to be available to visitors and supervise opening and security. Key holding, cleaning, booking and financial administration, health and safety and many other issues will need to be addressed much more than in a Sundays-only church. The ongoing running of the building is perhaps the most important aspect to address in deciding whether to go ahead with change.

Building adaptation: What, how, when?

Prepare a schedule of use for the new facilities. How many hours will the building be in use? This is best achieved by creating a grid that is a weekly timetable with the various slots during which the building will be used. Then fill in the name and user numbers of the various planned users. Footnotes can indicate whether these user groups are existing, currently asking for space or simply hoped-for. Proper preparation will result in the 'hoped for' being not just a twinkle in someone's eye but an unmet need in the local area with potential partners to provide a local service. Are there huge empty slots in the schedule? Often it is easier to fill a space on evenings and weekends, but will this be sufficient to justify change? Will a partially used hall bring in enough money to cover not just its maintenance but also regular repair and keeping facilities up to a high standard? If the church itself is being adapted for new uses, and if those groups and organizations use the building for more time than the church itself does, then those uses should be contributing more than the congregation does to maintenance and repair bills out of the total income. If this is not well planned, a financially hard-pressed congregation will be effectively subsidizing those other users.

Preparing a brief for the architect is described on p. 100, and the building works process is described on pp. 112–15.

Legal issues

During 2004 and 2005 the government is planning to introduce new licensing laws. These include a new provision that churches need not have a licence for activities other than worship. This exempts the church from entertainment licensing, but when the law happens the detail will need careful review. Performing rights, for example, should still apply, as this is the means by which music writers are paid for their work. Alcohol licences will still be needed, so if the new uses include for example a bar in the crypt, it will be important to have the right licence in place.[9]

The planning category or 'use-class' of churches allows for the church to be used for childcare or a health centre without additional planning permission, but all other kinds of use will need permission. Offices for the church's own use have always been included, but creating space that is dedicated to other use will almost always require planning permission. The church's architect should be able to advise on this.

If the church is planning, as a number have, to let a large area such as the crypt to a tenant who will run, for example, a restaurant then the tenant once selected may help in applying for the planning permission, but your architect will play a key role. Their business experience may enable them to answer questions more readily and decide more rapidly whether limitations set by planning officers will make the business impossible to run. Whenever a church is considering a long-term tenant, not only should the letting/lease/licence agreement be drawn

---

9 More information is available in *Managing your Community Building* from Community Matters, 8/9 Upper Street, London N1 0PQ or from Directory of Social Change.

up by a lawyer with commercial experience, but the tenant should be selected by competitive tender. Do not be afraid that the competition will frighten away a good potential tenant; businesses thrive on competition.

On all legal issues do seek the advice of a good ecclesiastical lawyer and if possible get additional help if the letting or lease is actually with a commercial company, as commercial law is different from church law. Consider advice from a lawyer from the charity sector who has helped charities with their commercial enterprises.[10] At present a church can only lease out part of its building by having the church made partially redundant. The Pastoral Measure before Synod (2004) will enable leases to be established under faculty. However, be very careful not to tie up valuable space in a long-term lease except in exceptional circumstances. Take advice before proceeding and ensure that the length of any lease is in the church's interests.

Value Added Tax

When a charity lets its building to others as a means of raising income this is considered an investment to utilize underused space, and not trading. That is, letting is similar to putting money in the bank and earning interest. If you would get more money by banking your asset as cash and not letting it out, that would be the preferred option of the charity commissioners, so the church should ensure that the investment of its assets in use for letting is in fact making real income. It is the responsibility of the church council as trustees to be good stewards of their assets, that is, to make the best possible return on assets in order to fund mission.

Value Added Tax becomes an issue when any non-religious activity is undertaken for profit, even if the activity is run in such a way that it does not make a profit.[11] A church café, social club, charity shop and bookshop may all need to register for VAT. If the activity turns over more than a certain sum (at present in the region of £45,000)

---

10 See Charity Pages from *The Directory of Social Change*.
11 This is a great simplification of a very complex structure. If there is any chance that the church should be registering, the advice of an appropriate accountant, VAT adviser or local VAT office should be sought.

registration is required. It is better to keep appropriate records than to discover after the fact that VAT returns should have been made, as the penalties are significant and all back-dated VAT has to be paid, whether collected by you or not.

A booklet is produced by the VAT office on VAT for charities.

Trading

Any activity that is neither the religious activity of the church/charity nor investment may be classified as trading. Running a café, social club, shop or concert programme are not religious activities and are therefore trading. They are not investment, as any return is based on commercial returns, that is, profit from the activity. Trading is not considered appropriate use of charity resources. Therefore in planning any non-religious activity that is not investment, the church should ensure it has an appropriate legal umbrella for carrying on the activity. Many trading activities can be run by a company wholly owned by the church council. This separates the risk of business from the normal charitable activity. All profits can still be dedicated to the church, all directors can be church members and the church council holds ultimate control of the company by owning the shares. A company is more easily controlled by the church council than a separate charity or charitable company, which would be controlled by the trustees and the objects of the charity and not by any outside group, even the church council. This is because the church council will be the corporate shareholder. However, seek the advice of a charity lawyer in setting up the company.

Do take note that the two entities, the church and the trading company, must be distinct, separately managed and financially independent. They may not at any level subsidize each other but must have open, clear and proper transactions between them. So the company pays rent for its office in the church and pays and manages its own staff. The connection is that the church council is the shareholder and the company pays rent and profit to the church. Two clear reasons for maintaining this legally required clarity are that the company will be subject to VAT but will not have to pay corporation tax on its donations to charity.

Both planning permission and faculty permission will be required before the trading activity can be set up; the former because a change of use is being planned and the second to ensure that the financial stability of the church is not being jeopardized by unwise or inappropriate developments.

Trading of various kinds to provide income requires careful preparation, not like a new charity project but in the same way that ordinary commercial businesses are set up. A church thinking of a trading activity should have the appropriate professional skills and support structures to ensure that the business is successful. Even if the profits will be dedicated to the church, it is not legally acceptable to invest the church's money in the business. The reason is that all the money donated to the church has been given to fulfil its religious purposes and therefore is restricted income. The business must be funded in other ways.

What safeguards are needed for a business venture creating income for the church? Clearly there is no such thing as a completely risk-free business, a business can lose money as well as make it. The business will be affected by incompetence or recession just like any commercial business, and incompetence in business can be present inside church as well as there being a difficult commercial climate for the business the church wishes to run. During recession restaurants and cafés tend to suffer more than other businesses, but in boom times they tend to do better! The only way to be as safe as possible is to be as prepared as possible.

First, *research and understand the business* you wish to start. Many charities run High Street charity shops, and while some make very good profits, others make almost nothing at all for all the volunteer time invested. Find people who have experience in the management and administration of such a business and seek their help in setting up.

Write a comprehensive business plan, just as if you needed to present the business to a bank for a start-up loan – even if you don't need to borrow from the bank.[12] Preparing the business plan will encourage realism, risk analysis and consideration of the financial expectations

---

12 See the chapter in *The UK Church Fundraising Handbook*, by Maggie Durran, Canterbury Press, 2003. Also *Creating and Managing New Projects*, Alan Lawrie, Directory of Social Change, 1996.

of a new business. If working capital is needed to start the business the church should get legal advice on whether and how it can lend that money to the business, without falling foul of charity law.

Ensure that the directors of the company working on such a business include the necessary business skills, but also include a cross-section of the church to ensure that the church has a good sense of ownership and commitment to the project as they will be crucial to accepting the business in the church, in helping and supporting in any difficult times and ensuring that the business operates with integrity and without undue risk.

Consider the potential customers for a commercial venture. Is there a gap in the local market for the business you have in mind? Are you in a location where such a venture will be able to pull in clientele?

Look at similar businesses in the area and see what they are achieving in terms of turnover and profitability. Other churches may be able to share their experience, so look at more than one. Remember every church business location is unique, your church will have both advantages and disadvantages in comparison with others. You will have your own set of problems to grapple with.

But do learn from the successes and failures of others, commercial or charitable, in your area. One church social club was convinced it could return to the profitability of a decade ago, but could not see that the local demographics and ageing population were working against it; over a period of five years with no pattern of review and change it came close to bankruptcy. It could not be supported financially by the church, as that would have been to use charitable funds to support the sale of alcohol, a clear violation of charity law. The club closed. Every business will have to review and upgrade itself if it is to remain profitable.

Especially in the case of church social clubs, the efficacy of the business should be thoroughly established and monitored. There are church social clubs where it is clear that managers and staff have followed a pattern common in the pub and bar industry, of pocketing some of the cash, and in cash-based businesses this is very hard to completely control. Particularly if the running of the social club becomes separate from the church and its culture of honesty, this becomes an issue. But even then, just as we have systems to protect our cash income in church (such as two people counting the cash from the church plate) there should be proper controls in the church business. Auditing the cash returns, the till rolls and the progress of stock will highlight many of the problems.

Finally, it is not always wise to set up the church members to run a business in order to make money from commercial enterprise. If the church has a suitable location for a business it may put the space out to tender for the kind of business wanted. An experienced trader will be a more stable business than a church group setting up for the first time. So various established companies, such as cafés or restaurateurs, may bid to lease the space. It may even be possible to negotiate for additional profit share or share of turnover as well as rent. In this way the church is assured income – rising income with a good lease – and takes very little of the risk.

Financial structure

The variety of activities that happen in the church with extended uses or with a busy church hall should be crystal clear in the book-keeping and accounting systems. Running a church hall, or running the church as everyday premises for use by a variety of groups, is investment, not religious activity, so this should be clearly identified in the accounts. Run a sub-account or separate page in the annual accounts for this activity. When hall accounts are incorporated into the ordinary church accounts of religious activity it can be hard to tell whether that other activity is really paying its way or whether church income, which by charity law should be spent on its religious activity (it is restricted), is being used to subsidize the aerobics group, the dog club, or the brownies and cubs by covering the real cost of their being in the building.

All trading activity, with the separate legal structure, must be run independently from the church accounts. If not, the VAT officer could make the decision that the regular church activity also has to be subject to VAT!

Management of specialized functions that are not the objects of the charity

Pastoral care or trading? Lots of churches are setting up a variety of outreach projects that they view as ministry more than trading in order to create income. If there is any doubt possible not just in the church's mind but in that of other people, then the best course of action is to seek the advice of the legal advisers in the diocese or at the charity commissioners. A café is one such case where the church may view its function as a context for evangelism, but whether it is viewed as such by the relevant authorities is a bigger question. The sale of religious books on a stall in church is Christian education and part of the role of the church in mission; but a bookshop serving coffee on the High Street may be seen differently. It is particularly important to clear the issue with the VAT office and set a separate financial and legal umbrella for any activity that is trading – even for evangelistic reasons – to ensure that the church does not discover too late that this is subject to VAT. There is a useful booklet on VAT for charities available from your local VAT office.

10

Running New Uses

Establishing a *vision* for an everyday church or busy church hall being open to and serving everyone in the neighbourhood is the first step. Getting the whole church's interest and commitment to the idea involves *leadership* (see p. 128). Making the project work effectively and efficiently to the benefit of everyone involves *management* – that is, a way of organizing resources to deliver the vision.

Much in the preceding chapters has been about how to organize the building itself; but just as significantly, finance, people's time and their skills will all need to be engaged productively for the vision to work out.

Finance

Even if the church is not preparing a business plan, it is crucial that the church council review the budget and cash flow projection for its new uses to ensure that financial integrity is maintained. Ideally the figures are looked at separately but alongside the church's main budget for its religious activity.

Over a period of five to ten years, will the everyday use contribute reasonably and realistically to the financial strategy of the church? Is there sufficient income to cover staff and utility costs? Is sufficient money coming in to cover building maintenance and repair and any other additional costs of having lots happening in the building? Consider the creation of a savings fund to cover major repairs in the future.

As the church reviews these income issues note that with a busy church with larger numbers of people coming and going, all the facilities will show wear and tear more quickly. Savings should be created that allow repairs and refurbishments to be done as needed. If the financial strategy does not create a fund for maintenance and repair, then in just a few years the church or hall will be shabbier and less attractive and become unused again. Good stewardship is needed of the building and finances.

Staff time

Assess the impact of the new uses on the time of existing staff and assess whether they have the necessary skills to take on the new work.

The clergy of the church may judge that they have some time and the skills, but few if any clergy – because of pastoral responsibilities – can be present at all the times access is needed for everyday activities.

Volunteers may prove both available and reliable. There are churches where too few people are available to make a regular commitment. Consideration can be given to employing staff to cover the necessary new roles. First, assess in detail the hours for which staffing is essential and consider part-time workers to cover these hours.

Skills

List the skills that are needed to complete the tasks that are being created. There are people who enjoy more defined and somewhat repetitive tasks and the day-by-day commitment and pride of place that is needed to keep church premises clean and well cared for.

More information is given on p. 135 about employing workers, but remember that Equal Opportunities law applies to church appointments, with some limitations in how it applies to clergy themselves.

Attention will need to be given to formulating the principles of the use of new facilities. Who will write the rules and guidelines, who will set up the financial procedures? And who will ensure that everything operates according to the guidelines?

Look at the guidelines in *Managing your Community Building* and at the *Purple Pack* from the Diocese of Southwark for more information (see Resources).

A church may find it helpful to set up a management committee functioning as a sub-committee of the church council. This will fit comfortably with having accounts that are presented as a separate sub-account in the church's annual accounts also. The church council will set the parameters or terms of this committee's work and receive reports on progress and copies of the minutes of its meetings. This means the detailed work of developing and managing new space does not load up the church council meetings where the focus of attention is rightly the worship, mission and ministry – the religious activity – of the church.

The church treasurer may have the right skills for setting up the book-keeping procedures for the everyday uses but often churches find that a part-time book-keeper on site and accountable to the treasurer is the best way to manage money.

Partnership

Churches in the past decade have experimented with a variety of partnerships that may provide increased use or increased income from their buildings. Sometimes partnership with another charity or community organization is the best way to attract investment from central or local government regeneration funds.

The structure of such partnerships often focuses on the revenue issues. Churches often provide the location and facilities and the partner organization the programme or activity. Whether this is as a weekly or annual letting the principles hold true that the contribution of the church must be properly recognized in the agreements and contracts involved.

Consider the cost to the partner organization of similar premises in the area. Consider the overheads involved.

A good breakdown is to look at a commercial model: a service charge plus rent:

A service charge is a direct charge to the 'tenant' organization of all the direct costs of their presence: maintenance, caretaking and cleaning, utilities, administration, any contracts for lifts or boilers and minor repairs. It may be best to proportion it out by the percentage of each week that each user is in the building.

Rent is calculated on a price per square foot or square metre basis and is a return to the owner for the use of the building. More about levels of rent is given on p. 74.

When the partner organization is funded by outside sources, regeneration or trusts, it is unnecessary to give an upfront rent-free period. A month or two may be acceptable *if the church can afford to cover this from its own funds*, but longer than that it becomes very difficult to establish the proper rent at a later date. The partner organization should never be released from the responsibility for the service charge. If the church is concerned that the partner organization is financially less stable and needs help, it sets a better principle if rent and service charge are collected from the organization and the church then makes its chosen donation to the organization.

Properly run community projects will normally have charitable status, have trustees responsible for their running, and a management committee that meets regularly to work out detail with the staff. A partner organization using the church may invite church members to join either its trustees or the management committee. This can be a very helpful arrangement that increases information and co-operation. However, remember that there will be issues that represent a conflict of interest, questions about rules and requirements of the church in the way the building is used, payment of charges due to the church, schedules of use and other issues. The management committee member who is also a church member should have a very clear understanding of the authority of the church council as stewards of the church's assets and facilities and not act against that in any way.

The risk analysis model in Appendix 1 may be used to facilitate the assessment of a potential partner organization as a tenant. The format will encourage the church to look realistically at potential partners. It will enable the church council to discuss the financial potential, staffing and resource implications and potential problems and address these with the potential partner.

Among the topics to consider and address with mitigating action are:

• Potential clashes with other users. For example, when children are in part of the building, can a project for the homeless including people who are affected by drugs, alcohol or mental illness be safely accommodated?

- Does the circulation area and signage within the church or hall facilitate use by more than one group?
- Can all the equipment and furniture needed by a partner be stored away so as not to interfere with the church's own activity?
- Does the partner present an increased security or safety risk?
- Are the facilities actually suited to this kind of use or is it a misfit that makes the provision less than good for the partner (in which case they will move on as soon as they find better premises)?
- Are they financially able to make a commitment to rent and service charges?
- Is the organization of good reputation with regard to its professional practice, the quality of service it provides, its staffing practice and its financial management?
- Is there a system for the church and the organization to work out teething problems about sharing premises?
- Good preparation around the principles of letting space will not only allay everyone's fears but also ensure much smoother relationships with those with whom the space is shared.

11

Letting or Leasing the Church or Hall

When a church is going to run a busy community facility in either the church or the hall, the first thing to address, even before considering raising the money to upgrade the facilities for general use, is how the new facilities in church or hall will be administered.

Scheduling

Running a facilities diary or weekly schedule is a straightforward activity but it requires meticulous care. Nothing kills a project more rapidly than double booking or the failure of a key holder to turn up as agreed.

In Appendix 3 a summary of a hall handbook (based on the *Purple Pack* of Southwark Diocese[13]) includes booking forms. For a busy building these are essential for the administrator to keep current with bookings that are taken when she/he is not present. Only bookings on the proper form are treated as valid and this lets everyone know where they stand. There should be no verbal bookings and no assumptions, even by the vicar! When the schedule includes church activity as well as lettings and outside events the combined schedule is critical to good administration. The lunchtime recital may be a problem for an event such as a funeral, that can never be predicted, but the clash can be dealt with constructively as long as the administrator gets the information at the earliest possible moment. Anticipated events of the church year can be entered on the calendar/schedule a very long time in advance and can be held open by the administrator and clashes thus

---

13 *Purple Pack*, Diocese of Southwark Communications Department.

avoided. Don't assume that the busy administrator will remember all the church calendar events from past years – book them properly.

The schedule should allow times for cleaning and caretaking to happen. For a busy hall this may be a daily requirement. Or equipment may be provided for each group to clean up after itself. Few groups will clean kitchens and toilets well, so these will still need to be done by someone who will do the job thoroughly and notice any repair and maintenance problems. Ask all groups to report any problems or repairs that are needed to the key holder when they leave. It is advisable to plan at least once each year to have no bookings for a week or two to allow for more major repairs and servicing.

A key holder or caretaker may be needed to unlock and lock up for each booking. It can become a huge problem if this is left to clergy who have many other pastoral demands to meet. If there are no reliable volunteer key holders available a paid caretaker may be prepared to work the anti-social hours that are often needed. Some organizations that have proved themselves responsible over a period of time may be their own key holder. But keep a very good record of who holds keys and has access. It is especially important that any key holding group does not drift into arriving early or leaving late, thus impinging on the time slot of another group.

Some groups need or require privacy and outsiders to the group may not be welcome, and that includes church members or staff. Under the Children Act non-group members may not go in and out of a space being used. An exercise class may feel uncomfortable with bystanders and a therapeutic group will not feel comfortable if overheard. Both the church and the group will need to feel comfortable with such arrangements and discuss such issues before a booking is made. An emergency may be an acceptable time for an interruption, but church members who are used to being able to have a free run of the building may find this restricting. Consider this issue with children's groups, exercise groups, women's groups, vulnerable elderly, therapy sessions, AA and others.

Terms and conditions for use of the space should be drawn up, including issues that may seem very obvious to church members. Notes on the content of terms and conditions are included in the appendices. Consider how introducing activity that is not worship may impact on the church itself.

- On which surfaces can objects be placed? Most churchgoers would feel uncomfortable with items being placed on the communion table, except for Christian worship. The font should not be used for placing or containing objects.
- Are there statues that should be protected?
- Are there places that should be off bounds?
- Should the floor or furniture be protected during certain activities? A children's activity workshop may be using glue and paper, what protection should be used?
- Performance of music or drama can mean moving heavy equipment. What can be moved how and what needs protecting? Items may not be 'bumped' up or down the front steps; the lift can take a maximum weight of x pounds; avoid bumping pillars or panelled walls.
- No nails or pins, Blu-Tack or self-adhesive tape, may be used on the fabric or fittings of the church. Notices may only be placed on existing noticeboards.

The church will have its own insurance for public liability but each group should consider its own insurance status. When letting space the church will be covered for the space and any accident that is caused by the negligence of church staff but not for the activity of the group and its leaders. Discuss all plans for changing use with the church's insurers.

Produce a straightforward set of rules that may be handed to every group and pinned to the noticeboard. Let groups know that breaking the rules is taken seriously. Groups may be banned from future use and all damage has to be paid for before deposits are returned.

Bookings to avoid

Some kinds of lettings and bookings are very hard on the facilities and have been banned by churches in their premises. Wedding receptions are the most commonly excluded. The reason has been that people at self-catering wedding parties seem to become so drunk that they are oblivious to the rules set, the closing time, noise and neighbours, and refuse to leave at closing time, making the job of the key holder/ caretaker almost impossible. A workable guideline may be to accept only those receptions where a catering company or event management company – who are working rather than partying – run the event and therefore act according to the church's guidelines.

Similarly, festival events with performances daily, stages being erected and scenery to manipulate may well cause damage, so special terms and conditions should be prepared to safeguard the building. When film companies hire spaces they often include clauses that provide for 'making good' for any wear and tear that results from their activity.

Any letting that may cause extra wear and tear can be asked to make a higher than usual deposit, and any refund of deposit is only made after all cleaning and repair is finished.

Letting to families and individuals

It is obvious that church events will be held in the church's extended facilities, but what about private events for church members, their families and friends. What concessions will be made?

Church events may need only to pay a fair share of utilities and overhead costs. Members and close friends may draw concessions, for example on the price, paying only the price set for church events. However, they should still keep to all the rules. Many of the rules are matters of health and safety and similar laws, and these should be kept by everyone. Though churches will not be covered by licensing laws, ending times and rules about noise and neighbours should be observed.

Fee levels for letting churches and halls

There are as many variations and ways of calculating this fee as there are churches in an area. However, here are some starting points.

Add up the following annual costs (you may wish to use a spreadsheet such as Lotus 123 or Excel for easiest analysis):

- Annual savings for long-term major repair.
- Annual cost of maintenance.
- Annual cost of minor ongoing repairs.
- Cleaning: supplies and staff time.

- Caretaking and key holding: equipment and time.
- Utilities.
- Insurance.
- Administration: materials, office and staff costs.

Divide this total by the total hours of letting per year and you have the running cost per hour. This gives the absolute minimum the church should charge without subsidizing the letting programme.

Then, investigate the cost of local community centres and halls in the area and find out their charges and limitations.

For most UK churches *with a busy programme* of lettings the rate is probably going to be a minimum of £20 rising to £25 or more. It may also be advisable to set several rates: one for the church's own use, one for community groups and charities and one for non-charitable and commercial activity. The latter rate can include local council use of space for local consultation or presentations, for commercial fitness trainers, for film companies, wedding receptions or any commercial venture.

Run a check, multiply out the income from letting the building at £25 for all groups and ensure this more than covers all the costs of running the hall. A facility used only spasmodically may not be able to pay for itself, in which case the entire strategy of lettings may need review! If the church is concerned that this is expensive for some groups to pay, once it is clearly making a surplus of income over expenditure and a contribution towards rent, then some groups may be given a concession. A small group of elderly pensioners on benefit may be charged less, and the same for a particular initiative with children. A rule of thumb is to divide the cost of the booking by the number of beneficiaries in the group to discover the cost per person. Now compare this cost with the other things members of the group spend money on. If it costs less than a drink at the pub for adults or less than a can of drink for children, they are probably getting a bargain!

There will always be groups who insist that they are a special case and should get a discount. Many arts groups happen to fall into this category. They, like any other charity, can get grants to cover their activity and it's the task of the church to fulfil its religious purpose; the church does not receive donations in order to subsidize theatre groups.

There are churches who find that daily rehearsals at a lower than normal evening rate help pay for the utilities and are better than no income. In order to avoid a pattern of giving away space at below cost, the committee might allow a concessionary rate on condition that if a properly paying booking comes along it will take precedence. Always charge something and always make everyone and every group pay in advance. Those with regular bookings such as every week should always pay monthly in advance.

Church facilities that are not being fully used by the church itself are considered as an asset that may be let out to make income to sustain the mission of the church. If the facilities are used to benefit any activity other than the religious objects of the church, then they are being used to further the objectives of other charities or organizations. Under charity law this is not proper use of the asset, which has to be dedicated to the objects for which it was given in the first place. To let out facilities – for good causes – and to make an income from those lettings to further the church's objects, is investment. Therefore breaking even or just covering the costs is not enough; the facilities should be producing the service charge, that is running costs, plus a reasonable rent to the church.

Long-term leases

Under current church law in the Church of England consecrated buildings may not be leased out; they are only licensed for other use. During 2004 and 2005 there may be a change in the law allowing a minority of space to be leased to a tenant on something like a commercial lease. But before going in that direction the church needs to take comprehensive advice from the diocese and legal advisers about the implication of tying up church space for a number of years (see p. 110). There may in future be a change in mission or management of the church that results in the need for space, and the lease or licence must bear this in mind. There are churches that in a time of slow growth or depression let out space, which may again be needed for ministry when a new and more dynamic minister is engaged.

For church space, such as halls, that are vested in the church council, leases may be drawn up using a commercial lawyer, remembering that members of the church council are still responsible as trustees for ensuring that this is done properly and in the best interests of the church. Such leases may be subject to approval by the diocesan board of finance. The church building is not normally vested in the church council, unless it is classified as redundant, and licences for using the consecrated space in the church are subject to faculty, and that includes approval by the archdeacon and others in authority; they should be drawn up by an ecclesiastical lawyer.

The most significant steps prior to setting up a lease are:

- A far-reaching and thorough review of mission and ministry and the potential needs of the church to use its own space.
- Preparing the heads of terms and negotiating with the proposed tenant to agree these before leases are drawn up and signed.

Review of mission and ministry needs for space

Leases under the Landlord and Tenant Act are usually constructed with break clauses. That is periodically, usually every five years, the lease may be broken by the owner if the space is required for their own use, not for re-letting. So the church must review at what point they might need to reuse the space themselves and ensure that the shaping of break clauses in the lease is reasonable. In fact the church should consider that for the length of the lease they will not require the space, the break clause is for exceptional circumstances. In parallel, the lease should contain a five-yearly rent review as well as annual increases in line with inflation.

Many churches really do have excess space, but quantifying how much is excess and what additional space they may need to reserve has to be carefully planned. It is better that space that the church may need in the near future is let out on an occasional basis rather than leased.

Consider the following:

1 Although the church has normal requirements from week to week, are there occasional times or events for which the church needs to expand into additional space? For major funerals or memorial services, Christmas or New Year, Holy Week or other events? Are

there spaces which are not used at all by the congregation or for the church's ministry?

2 Is there likely to be increased need for work with children for Sunday School or crèche for which small rooms ancillary to the main worship area are needed? Assess carefully, being realistic, as it takes time and the right skills and commitment to build up a Sunday School where none currently exists.

3 Are there social or care groups run by the church that need space on Sundays or other days? How much space do they really need? – Quantify this, and in the planning for releasing under-used space to create income, consider consolidating uses so that what may have spread all over the building may be consolidated in one meeting room or in the church itself, making others available for letting.

4 Are there major building works planned in the near or medium future that would impact on space that you wish to lease? Having leased the space it is not easy to take it over for repair work that interferes with the tenant's business without compensating the tenant for their loss of business. This may affect the time at which a lease can begin.

5 If the building is going to undergo major repairs that do not necessarily impact directly on the tenant's space the impact should still be assessed. Builders on scaffolding may be using noisy equipment and so impact on the tenant. At the very least such work should be recognized at the beginning of the process.

Having looked at the needs and issues around underused facilities, the next step is to summarize your findings and consult with diocesan advisers and property departments. With their expertise in advising churches their advice may make a contribution you cannot afford to miss. The legal department will also be able to offer advice on the way the development with potential tenants is handled.

Heads of terms

The heads of terms in preparing a lease are usually represented in an exchange of letters between the two parties, agreeing the general terms so that the lawyers from both sides can work out the detail. *Until* your lawyer tells you a tenant can take up residence do not give the tenant keys or control of the space: however desperate the church may be for money, the legal situation will be a nightmare! In particular, letting tenants in without an agreement is by default an agreement and the church will not like the default terms!

Key terms you should consider are:

1 Cost per annum of rent and probable service charge. The rental should be determined by two factors. The first is the going rate for similar facilities in the area represented by a price per square foot or square metre per annum. And the second is calculated by the capital value of the space or building multiplied by a reasonable interest charge if that were money in a deposit account. (The latter is of interest because the church as a charity has a responsibility to make the best possible return on its assets in order to support its ministry.) The service charge covers the cost of utilities, repairs and maintenance. In addition, if the church has to employ a caretaker or other staff to service space or serve functions from which the tenant benefits, such as dealing with rubbish or cleaning, then a proportion of their cost should be added to the service charge.

2 Any other costs to which the tenant should or could contribute, such as repairs and maintenance, and cleaning of common areas.

3 The extent of insurance should be part of this agreement. The church's responsibility as the building's owner results in them insuring the structure and having public liability, but the extent to which the tenant insures their own staff and their own activities should be agreed. The tenant should be responsible for their own contents unless their loss is clearly caused by the church's negligence. In addition the church should have insurance in case something happens which prevents the tenant carrying on their business in the building; usually this will involve an unforeseeable repair or maintenance problem that interrupts use of the building.

4 The length of the tenancy and any break periods. Most agreements require tenants to leave the space in good repair when the tenancy ends or to pay compensation for work that is needed. The length of tenancy should be reasonable with regard to the church's own need and be reasonable on the leasing market; that is, a really short lease will only be marketable to business that can easily load up its

furniture and move to a new space. It will not work for businesses that are location-sensitive, that is, if they advertise and win custom on the basis of their location, or if the business itself requires the installation of equipment, such as a commercial kitchen.

5 The various responsibilities for repair and making good. The tenant may be responsible for keeping their entire space in good working order and up to standard with regard to internal decoration. It may be subject to occasional visits by the church or an agent to ensure this is being done, and written notice of such visits would be expected.

6 The church's responsibility for the structure of the building and any shared facilities and the standard to which the church will maintain those facilities.

7 Under what terms might the owner have emergency access to the tenant's space?

8 Any common entrance space and how it may be used. Are there any limits on use of the entrance by the tenant or the church including opening times in the morning and closing-down times in the evening?

9 Behaviour. Are there acceptable or unacceptable levels of noise by either church or tenant? Consider the noise of equipment or radios in an office or practising the organ in church. The latter when heard endlessly for several hours can be a severe problem to a quiet office. Additionally, there may be hours during which noise should not be made but other times when it does not matter. (For example, that church services should not be disturbed by extraneous noise, but later in the evening in a detached church building, noise may be made without problem.)

10 Utilities. The extent of utilities installed by the client should be agreed. On most buildings the routes of cables and pipes should be subject to all the processes of architectural oversight (by the church's inspecting architect, whose time for this purpose will be paid for by the incoming tenant) and faculty and planning permission. Installation of anything that is to be fixed to the walls or ᵗʰerwise attached to the building should be subject to agreement ᵗot to be unreasonably withheld. On listed buildings the pipes and cables should be thoroughly discussed at ᵉ to ensure that archaeological and other implications

are considered properly. Often they are not insuperable, but early consideration can save some major problems.

11 Since all shared buildings run into problems between user groups at times, the way that problems will be resolved should be set up at the outset. Many problems will be solved by staff but others may need some arbitration by an outside person or professional agreeable to both parties.

12 Rent increases. Rent increases should happen at least at every break clause period, but it is preferable, having agreed the initial level, to increase annually by inflation as a matter of course and then have a professional review every three or five years, by a chartered surveyor, to ensure that the level corresponds to market rents in the area.

13 Any other areas your lawyer recommends for inclusion.

14 Some dioceses have staff or advisers who can help a local church with these issues. Additionally, visit other churches who have successfully achieved this change and explore with them the lessons they have learned, the legal advice that they found most constructive and the financial return they have made to support their mission.

12

Community Projects and their Sustainability

Many churches, in creating additional programmes in their under-used buildings, plan to add a community project, which usually means running a project that caters in some way for those who are disadvantaged and for whom there are less than adequate facilities already in the neighbourhood. This section is an introduction to the work and the issues involved. If this is the direction your church wishes to go, then thorough preparation guidelines are available from the Diocese of Southwark in the *Purple Pack*, Parts One to Four.[14]

First assess the availability of people with the necessary *skills and time* for managing a new community project.

Some projects can be started by unskilled volunteers, for example a drop-in facility for refreshments and friendship. For a children's programme it is helpful even for a drop-in parent-and-toddler play session to have some volunteers with relevant experience.

Any time children will be under the care of an adult other than a parent or legal guardian a police check is required to ensure that the carer is a suitable person to have oversight of children. Most dioceses are developing and establishing significant work under this sphere of the Children Act so that all those who are entrusted with the care of children in church, or are most likely in virtue of their role to be trusted with the care of children, are vetted through the criminal checking procedure. No corners should be cut on this process, as those who would abuse children look and behave just like the rest of us in public; it is only in secret that their behaviour becomes abusive.

---

14 Available from Diocese of Southwark Communications Department.

At a parent-and-toddler session the child's carer is still in charge of the child, but in all other occasions in church groups with children and vulnerable young people, sessions should be held to train and establish good practice by workers, volunteers and group leaders. For example, it is important to agree the ways in which to deal with children's bad behaviour (such as returning them to their parents!); to ensure a register is kept at all sessions and to have an accident book and basic first aid skills.

Projects for adults that include advice or education, uniformed organizations, or youth and sports activity will require some trained input in management and development. Since in these latter cases the project will almost always employ professionally qualified people, those on the management committee will need sufficient skill to develop the programme with an appropriate level of expertise.

The *time* required to run a well-established community project is commonly a management committee once each month. There will be additional time spent by the chairperson and by key members such as secretary and treasurer on particular relevant aspects. During the setting up of a new project, more meetings will be essential and committee members may need time also to meet staff of other organizations in the area that are important to the church's own project development; this may include council officers of the community development and social services departments.

If the project is not to be fully funded by the church itself then strategic planning will necessarily be followed by a period of *fundraising*. The more that funding is sought from outside the church itself, the more that the strategy and objectives of the project will have to be compatible with the aims of outside funders. On the whole a community project with a religious objective can be funded by the church (and this may be the only potential source of funds). If the church community project is designed to serve the welfare, education or health needs of local people it is best established under a separate charitable structure with its own trustees, and the church's contribution can be made as a charitable donation. Any community project that hopes to get funding from non-religious sources will need to have its management, finances and programme clearly separate from the church's religious activity. Detailed preparation for fundraising for community projects in included in Chapter 11 of *The UK Church Fundraising Handbook*.[15]

Adequate professional skills are required for most community programmes. Outside funders will expect and require that the projects that they fund be of the best possible professional practice. For this professional training and experience are required more than just Christian good will. Having well-intentioned members will not substitute for professional training. Equally a community project will be subject in every way to Equal Opportunities legislation: it is not legal to set up a project that plans to employ social workers, for example, and make those jobs available only to members of the church. On pp. 136–8, under managing people, a section is included on using Equal Opportunities practice in employing staff.

Sustainability

When setting up a project that is based on outside funding bear several issues in mind with regard to sustainability.

1 The project should pay its fair share of rent and service charge for use of the facilities of the church. If the church wants to offer financial support it is preferable to set and receive the rent and service charge and then make a donation to the project. This keeps very clear the contribution that the church has committed to the project, and if times get harder financially then the church's priorities can be more readily assessed.

2 Funding from outside sources, especially from trusts, can be short- or medium-term. Sometimes grants are for three years, and occasionally, as with the National Lottery, that can be renewed for a further three years maximum. Therefore, however good the community project, church members may need to be prepared to end the project when the money runs out. For this, good review procedures should be in place and proper financial planning be made for redundancy of staff. If the church has come to depend on the rental income, then alternatives should be planned.

---

15 See *The UK Church Fundraising Handbook*, Maggie Durran, Canterbury Press, 2003.

3 The project should be regularly and rigorously reviewed to ensure that the standards are maintained at a high level and with integrity. Failure to do so can result in the church itself getting a bad reputation in the area and will run against future support for church community projects. Weak projects with poor working practice are often continued by churches, as they like to be kind to everyone, including workers who are failing to achieve the aims of the project. This is a good reason for having a separate management committee.

4 Develop an annual review of cashflow for the building and its projects. Undertake a risk analysis that is updated annually for the church, its community projects, lettings to groups and individuals, and any projects with a longer lease or licence. This will enable the church in its now busier everyday existence to foresee financial problems, address negative trends and improve on winners.

13

Visitors

Increasingly, and if only to respond to the requirements of funders of listed church buildings, we are seeking more ways to leave buildings open to the general public. In busy urban areas where churches are in the town centre, many people drop in for quiet and prayer. In other places people are on heritage trails and are looking at our past and our story as seen in the building. Whether our highest concern is developing mission or being available to the public who have helped provide finance for repair, it is to our advantage to be open for visitors.

Making the building secure

Various churches have found ways to supervise opening for visitors. I still find village churches that simply open the doors each morning and lock up in the early evening with no security provision other than putting away the silver, without negative impact. Urban churches have adopted several approaches to remain both secure and open to visitors.

The Open Churches Trust has supported some Grade I churches in having a rota of volunteers to be on duty, giving information and help to visitors and also to sound the alarm if a problem occurs. (Usually the presence of someone on duty is deterrent enough.)

Additionally, churches commonly have security pressure pads under any valuable or risky items from candlesticks to ancient chests, so that if they are moved an alarm goes off. Of course, the cheap and relatively valueless candlesticks are the ones left out.

People on site also deters arsonists – for some reason they like churches, and we now commonly have stands of candles alight and money boxes for donations – so providing them with the tools of their trade! A fire/smoke alarm should always be installed.

Contrary to frequent perceptions, the Ecclesiastical Insurance Group do not require that churches be kept locked and actually recognize that churches that are kept open can be safe provided reasonable precautions are taken.

In the City of London churches are increasingly installing CCTV so that staff in the church office have a constant overview of what is happening and can go into the church itself if someone appears to be acting strangely. It is less costly than paying for staff and the location is not amenable to finding volunteer staff.

In other churches there are church offices with windows looking into the church, so that there is supervision.

Whichever method you use, undertake a risk analysis, thinking of all the things that may go wrong, and systematically plan for how the church may best ensure they don't. Consider removing or fixing down large valuable items and putting pressure pads under others.

Consider the fire risk and ensure both the alarms and the fire extinguishers are in order and everyone knows how to use them. Put up a notice telling people what to do next if a fire or burglar alarm is activated. Avoid heroism, watch but do not intervene when there may be an intruder and call out the professionals: dial 999 for the police or the fire brigade.

Train your volunteer church watchers in caring for visitors and dealing as safely as possible with crises.

Do ensure that keys are kept safely and that as few people as possible have keys. Keep an up-to-date record of key holders, with their contact details.

Directions, signs and notices

Protection may be improved if an obvious sign tells people that CCTV is in operation, but signs and notices are important to all visitors.

Start with directions to the church if its location is not obvious. In rural areas, there may be a need for a signpost on the main road, where the village has over the centuries moved away from its focus on the church. Some local authorities in urban and inner-city areas will erect direction signs to notable local churches and places of worship.

Welcome. Not all visitors speak English and the more urban the location the more likely it is that non-English speakers will visit. Some research is needed into the church's particular catchment of visitors, but on the whole if we never welcome those of other languages and other faiths in a manner they can understand, it may not be surprising that they don't visit. The main welcome sign can be in many languages without being site-specific. It may be time for dioceses to bear the cost of getting such notices designed and made so that local churches have only to find the cost of mounting the printed sign.

Consider welcome leaflets in several languages, and to make the cost more bearable a deanery or group of churches could share a multi-language leaflet with general information about each of them and what people can expect in visiting a Christian place of worship.

Help people know how to behave in your building. I often feel intimidated and I know what happens, so how difficult it must be for the unchurched. I see them creeping around the edges of the space not knowing what they can do. So prepare a leaflet that introduces people to how the building is used (include pictures of worship in progress) and explain the font, the lectern, the pulpit and the table. Explain what is more precious or should not be touched, but also tell people what to do to make the most of their visit. Invite them to take time to pray, light a candle and so on. Most churches already have some kind of printed historic guide to the building, but this should be only one of several as visitors are introduced to the living as well as the historic church. A clear notice should invite visitors to join worship, and give the time of the next service. Daily offices and lunchtime services are an important witness for churches with lots of drop-in visitors.

Signage may be needed to help visitors find and identify obscure or hidden features of interest.

Many churches now have clear and helpful noticeboards that include pictures of church officers and how they may be contacted.

Boundaries

If we never tell people what we do and do not have available, or what we have the resources to offer, it is not surprising that failing their expectations becomes an issue.

With visitors coming into the building, it is quite easy to put a rope across the chancel steps or near to the communion table if we wish them to be avoided. It can be very offensive to most Christians if a backpacker puts their bag on the communion table while peering at carvings or murals. Most people will respond positively to the rope, or to a small sign that says that nothing may be placed on the table.

Where a city centre church attracts people who are on the edges of society and may be mentally ill or otherwise socially dysfunctional, creating boundaries may be extremely important to personal safety. It is worth having a sign that the church never hands out money under any circumstances, and ensuring that absolutely everyone keeps to the rule. By all means give out small quantities of food or tell people where they may get food or claim state benefit. If some people do not keep the money rule there will be problems, as the drop-in beggar will believe that that they are being slighted and that if they only get more persistent and demanding they will get what they want. The word soon gets around among people on the street that a certain church is or isn't a good place to beg. Consistently saying no does help the situation.

In my own experience as a parish priest I kept the money rule, but also had a supply of tins and jars from the harvest giving so that people who claimed hunger could be provided with help. Since churches do not so often give money, the requests on my doorstep were more often for fares to 'Mum's funeral'. I was at first suspicious and felt guilty for not giving any money, but when six months later the same man returned with the same story I knew that the 'fare' would be spent in a local off-licence and I had made the right decision. My mantra was and is that it is not a charitable act to give or provide people with alcohol.

For my own security, when a clearly dysfunctional person appeared in church or at the vicarage door I made sure that I was not in an enclosed space with them on my own. I did not invite them into the vicarage where I was alone, but moved outside with them towards the street where others might be aware if violence or aggression broke out. In church I moved where others could see what was occurring, out into the street if necessary. I also had an agreement with church members that I would keep talking to difficult visitors but it was their job to call the police (999) if they had any reason to think that the situation was not safe. Having previously worked in a project for women survivors of domestic violence, I always made proper plans and calming down potential aggression my concern.

Health and safety

While it is covered more fully elsewhere (see p. 21), the health and safety of visitors should be looked at carefully and as part of a thorough analysis of risks. Church members may be familiar and relatively safe with items such as the boiling urn for tea-making in the corner of the nave. But visitors with children may not. If you create a 'kitchen corner' in church, the rules about its use must be the same as for a kitchen (see p. 25) and barriers created that mean children may not get near to the danger of hot water.

Tea and coffee-making and washing-up must not be undertaken in ways that risk health and safety. Helpers must be able to wash their hands away from preparation space, especially after using the toilet. If washing-up facilities are limited, use only disposable cups and cutlery. I still find churches where the mouse in the church kitchen is tolerated, and other abysmal standards that people would not have in their own homes are tolerated.

Cable runs should be protected; steps should be highlighted and handrails tested and checked. All hazards that are unavoidable should have warning signs.

If there are cupboards of cleaning materials these should be locked and have a chemical hazard warning sign displayed.

The toilets must be clean and hygienic. A notice should be displayed telling what to do in the case of fire or other emergency. People from other countries do not automatically think of 999 for police, ambulance or fire brigade, so display the number clearly.

Have an honest and thorough review of the health and safety of visitors and set up an action plan for dealing with the identified issues.

Attracting visitors

Does your church have an informative website that tells visitors when they might visit and find the church open? It must be up to date and attractive. Many churches have helpful volunteers who are good at technology; but do look at the content and accessibility of information through the eyes of a stranger. Is welcome its first message?

Opening hours should be appropriate to the visitor, and weekends are always popular in small towns and villages while weekdays may be more important in cities. City centre churches strive to be open every day!

Heritage walks or tours. Guidance leaflets may be developed by groups of churches in an area so that visitors can be attracted to the area.

Promotion can happen in a number of ways that reflect the variety of reasons that people might visit a church, anything from heritage to evangelism. The methods of communication and the locations of advertisements must reflect where the visitor will look. Local councils are increasingly developing visitor leaflets, and churches should make enquiry, preferably before those leaflets are devised, in order to feature. Public buildings may have leaflet displays for visitors, and church visitor information may be displayed there with permission.

Many holiday resorts have publications targeted at visitors, in hotels and other accommodation. Ensure that your church is listed both as a heritage visitor location and for the programme of services that are available. It may be advisable to mention your churchmanship for visiting worshippers seeking something with which they are familiar.

And, of course, use events from church fêtes to cream teas, concerts and flower festivals to create opportunity for people to visit the church and meet the people.

Part 3

Major Building Projects

14

Preparing for Major Building Projects

Most clergy – and most church councils – face a major building project just once in their working life. When it happens, the building
project seems to take over clergy time to the exclusion of most of their
usual work. It is essentially a time-consuming task, leading the church
and church council through a period of change and interruption, with
clergy being the key link with the design team as the project progresses. The task is made infinitely more difficult by the fact that most
clergy have no preparation or training in what to do, what to expect
and how to safeguard the church's interests and make sure the work is
completed in the most effective and efficient way possible. What follows in this chapter is an attempt to summarize that process, one that
I have only learned about by doing, and this summary is therefore only
as broad as my experience and only as clear as the understanding I
have gained on several major building projects. It may be helpful to
use this process that follows as an outline to run through with the
church council (or with the churchwardens) and later with the
church's architect, to make your own map of what is going to happen
and what each person/role will achieve at each step of the way.

What is the need?

1 Major repairs are identified in the church's Quinquennial Inspection report. Normally inspecting architects give a timescale for the
  period during which such works should be undertaken. Repair to
  roofs, water disposal and other structural works may not be able to
  wait, as the weather may cause further damage and water will eventually get in to damage the church interior. Other kinds of work,
  such as the repair of what is aesthetic rather than structural, may

wait longer. The money has to be raised before major works can be undertaken, so the timescale of preparing for repair works will include fundraising, which is not addressed in this book.[16]

2 Alterations to a church in order to allow for additional uses may represent the need, and in this case the church should prepare a description of the needs to be met in the use of the building, times of use, numbers to be catered for, facilities that are required. (See Figure 14.1.) Often there is a financial need as well as a ministry agenda driving the plan for alteration and it is important to prepare sufficient financial projections to ensure that this is a realistic and viable way to develop financial sustainability. For example, how many people from the church's catchment area want to or can attend concerts at the suggested price, and is this sufficient return on the capital investment of altering the space to accommodate them? Other uses may be more in demand, and in addition to producing a better income may serve local people more effectively.

3 For a church hall refurbishment the uses to which the hall is already put, or the needs for meeting space by people and organizations in the neighbourhood, may represent the need. In this case the uses, numbers, times and types of user groups all should be quantified to help the design work fit the actual need. Very often church halls (and sometimes churches) have been designed with lots of toilet stalls to allow for occasional maximum use of the space, and that happens only once or twice a year; in fact other facilities are needed more and smaller toilet facilities would have been fine. So fill in a chart as Figure 14.1 suggests.

Be careful not to overestimate need. Often churches think they want a large catering kitchen, only to find it is used only occasionally, and that a much smaller kitchen would do for those events and a church office could have been fitted in alongside it. Be very realistic about the numbers involved. One church hall in London needed a kitchen for most groups every day, but only to make drinks and serve biscuits and snacks; a large kitchen would have only been used at anything near capacity once or twice a year. Is it worth allocating expensive space to a large under-used kitchen?

---

16 See *The UK Church Fundraising Handbook*, Maggie Durran, Canterbury Press, 2003.

Figure 14.1 Brief for St Mark's Community Hall

Activity	Current location	Average numbers	Maximum numbers	Time	Special requirements	Location issues	Comments
Sunday							
Children's parties	L H	50	50	pm			Refreshments preparation
Children's parties	S H	25	25	pm			Refreshments preparation
Sunday School	S H	4	10	am			
After church refreshments		50	70	am			Additional to present hall use
Monday							
Kidsworks	L H	30	30	am			Refreshments preparation
Luncheon club (new)		20	25	Noon +pm		kitchen	Additional to present hall use
Table tennis	L H	10	15	eve			
Playgroup	S H	30	30	am			Refreshments preparation
Beavers	S H	24	30	eve			
Scouts	S H	30	30	eve			

H = Large Hall S H = Small Hall

continued

Activity	Current location	Average numbers	Maximum numbers	Time	Special requirements	Location issues	Comments
Tuesday							
Aerobics	L H	120	50	am			Refreshments preparation Come & go during am
Table tennis	L H	10	15	eve			
Social group	S H	25	30	am			
Elderly fellowship	S H	12	15	eve			
Wednesday							
Aerobics	L H	120	50	am			Refreshments preparation Come & go during am
Luncheon club (new)		20	25	Noon +pm		kitchen	Additional to present hall use
Bingo (elderly)	L H	35	40	eve			Refreshments preparation
P. & toddlers	S H	20	25	am			Refreshments preparation
Venture Scouts	S H	20	25	eve			
Thursday							
Kidsworks	L H	30	30	am			Refreshments preparation
Tai chi	L H	25	30	eve			
Playgroup	S H	30	30	am			Refreshments preparation
Cubs	S H	35	40	eve			

Friday							
Aerobics	L H	120	50	am			Refreshments preparation Come & go during am
Luncheon club (new)		20	25	Noon +pm		kitchen	Additional to present hall use
Martial arts	L H	25	30	eve			
Playgroup	S H	30	30	am			Refreshments preparation
Saturday							
Parties	L H	35	50	am/pm		kitchen	
Parties	S H	30	35	am/pm		kitchen	
Social events	L H	120	120	eve	Occasional	kitchen	

Additional notes

1. Parish office at the front with a view of the entrance.
2. The new building should adjoin the church to produce optimum use of the facilities.
3. Glass doors allowing people to see into the church when they come for activities and vice versa.
4. More groups need refreshments preparation than a kitchen (warming kitchen) and an additional drinks machine would appeal to other groups.
5. Space would be used for coffee after church.
6. Any space may be locked off from the circulation area when any individual space is in use.
7. Budget is approximately £500,000.
8. If a children's group is in the main hall, it will be helpful (under the Children Act) for that group to have access to the toilets and no other. If small hall is also booked can one toilet, for example, the disabled accessible toilet, be available to that group's use?

Developing the brief

For major church repairs the brief from the client to the design team (architect and other key professionals) may be very straightforward in replacing like with like. However, the church will wish to determine the extent of the works. Repairs to stonework, for example, could include stones essential to the structure, or stones that are badly worn, or stonework that will not last more than ten years. The difference between the scopes of each of these definitions may be tens of thousands of pounds. What the church can afford will be a key factor. Repairs that are essential to the integrity of the building, in remaining wind and watertight may have to be included and fundraising got under way, while other works can be left for another time.

For alterations and refurbishment to churches and church halls or a new building there are many more elements to the preparation.

Consider each of the following.[17]

The longevity of the building. The effort of raising lots of money to build something with a short life can be very depressing for church members who will still be here in twenty years when the building begins to fail. It is usually preferable to ask for a building of traditional long-lasting materials. Such a building will also generate local pride and enhance the environment.

A long-term view may also mean that detailed design for one specific group's needs should be readily reversible in the future. With demographic changes, there may be no need for a nursery school in the future – do the fixtures and fittings mean the room is ill-suited to other uses?

Designing facilities that are accessible to the disabled. Toilets, doorways, kitchen, activity space should all be designed to accommodate everyone who might come to the building, including wheelchair users. Lighting, signage, induction loops and other supports and guidance should take into account the needs of people who are deaf, or have impaired sight or other disabilities.

---

17 See *Village and Community Halls*, Guidance from the National Lottery distributing bodies, 1996.

Location. People will more readily use a building if it is easy to get to, they can easily park cars, and it is attractive and there are no perceived hazards in approaching it. If the church has choice in siting a new building, such issues are critical to the successful inclusion of new people.

Planning approval. The architect will be responsible for gaining the necessary permissions for the final design, but bear in mind that local authority agreement for building work in and around a listed building or in a conservation area may be more difficult to get.

Ownership. Many church properties and land are not yet registered with the land registry and this is a useful point at which to get this relatively straightforward measure in place. The diocesan registry will help. If the church is going to outside sources for funding this is an essential step.

Outside facilities. Is the church creating any parking space, even a drop-off facility for those with wheelchairs? Eventually this may be a vital issue with the local authority, who are responsible for avoiding traffic problems. The architect will consult them, but explore what the church would like as a starting-point, after which negotiation with the local authority can take place.

Character of the building. This applies not only to new buildings, but to refurbishment also.

- *The look of the building in its locality.* Should it look modern or like older buildings around? Should the materials be traditional or modern, does the church like glass and steel or brick and stone? Ideally the design, modern or older, will still be high quality even when unadorned.
- *Appropriateness to the purpose.* Taking account of the kinds of groups and their needs and their numbers that will use the spaces. It will need to feel homely to some groups, but others simply want a large space for vigorous activity. Research on the usual and maximum numbers in various user groups will facilitate this process.
- *Relation of rooms to each other.* Who needs the kitchen and at what times? When children are in the main hall, because of the Children Act, the toilet facilities may need to be unavailable for the use of other people.

- *How do people need to circulate between rooms and facilities?* Are there aspects or room arrangements that would create difficulties? For example, all rooms may need to access the toilets or the kitchen, without going through a space that is being used by another group. How many people arrive at one time, and can the lobby/foyer cope with the numbers?
- *What services are needed?* Heating, lighting, ventilation, security and fire alarms systems, fire exits and ways for access to be controlled as necessary?
- *Additional accommodation.* Storage; types of chairs and tables and their storage; storage of special items such as sports equipment; the outside tap that can take a hosepipe; a flower room to serve the church; each and every special item should be considered and negotiated into the design.

When alterations are planned to an historic building, especially one that is listed or in a conservation area, not only are the needs for new use to be considered, but the nature of the building and its care and conservation are factors that the church and the architect must take into account. The design must minimize the impact on historic fabric and design, and for internal works it should be reversible. External works should be seen to be a worthy twenty-first-century addition to the building. Today's congrgation may find their building uncomfortable, bewildering, over-large and even unsightly, but if it is of historic significance that significance cannot be ignored. A good architect can go a long way towards meeting the needs of the contemporary church without violating the historic design. Having a long-term view that recognizes that a future generation may have yet another set of needs can ensure that appropriate care is taken in how changes are made in the building.

As ideas are drawn together, and the architect begins to grapple with the design, it is very helpful to plan a period of *local consultation*. Those who live nearby may eventually object to planning permission or listed building consent. Talking to them early may result in incorporating their interests and concerns (those may be very useful contributions) and give an easier passage through the planning permission process.

Legislation is being prepared by the government that includes the exemption of all churches from being licensed for entertainment.

Church halls will still need licences but will not need to pay for them. The Public Entertainment licence governs the safety of the premises for events and the prevention of public nuisance. If the hall is used only for letting to activity groups, this will not be needed, but for any public display, performance, sports event, dancing or music event the licence will be needed. The licence will dictate the closing time, set up health and safety restrictions and control the number of people allowed in. For a small number of theatre performances in church a licence will not be needed, but the licensing authority must be notified for plays, ballets and such, as fire, safety and seating arrangements have to be approved. Similarly, church halls will not have to pay the fee normally involved in such checks.

Alcohol licences are needed whenever alcohol is sold. A charity cannot hold an alcohol licence without potentially violating its charitable status (and a church is a registered charity without a charity number) as selling alcohol is not a charitable activity. Occasional licences or club licences may be acceptable. For specific events a local publican may work as a partner with an extension to the pub's licence.

Managing the project

Delivering good quality building works to an acceptable programme and an agreed budget is not a lucky break but the result of good management. In the author's experience, several churches that have professional project management skills or experience have chosen to employ outside professional project management for their building works, and several with little experience have opted to manage the project themselves. What are the pros and cons?

Historically, architects have functioned as project managers more often than not. The church as client needs a good manager, but the architect's focus before the construction phase begins is on design and quality, using the quantity surveyor to inform on the cost of the resultant design. On many works there is a way to change the design or limit the scope of works to restrict expenditure, but the amateur client often will not know how to do this but accepts the price as fixed. During the construction phase, with its focus on function and quality of work, despite the agreed tender price, the costs can escalate. A dedicated project manager can address the cost issue at all stages, and when an item may of necessity go over cost the manager can require a cutback elsewhere.

Should the church choose to employ a professional project manager, and what can this professional take on? A professional project manager often comes from a quantity surveying background and should be registered as a member of the Institute of Project Managers. If someone already in or known to the church takes on this role as volunteer, it is advisable to check out their skills and credentials just as thoroughly as when interviewing outside professional project managers. It is very difficult to take issue with a volunteer church member whose hold on the project slips or is less than effective. It may be better to have members with related skills on a committee that liaises with the project manager; fellowship is less likely to be damaged.

For smaller or straightforward projects, or if the church has long experience with an architect and knows that the person normally keeps to agreed costs and timescales as well as to quality of work, then the project manager may be an unnecessary professional on the team. Architects who are unfamiliar with having project managers on board may not like the structure very much, preferring the more traditional system of controlling everything themselves. Again, if the church prefers this more traditional route, interview the architect about the requirements of a project's management, and expect the architect to tell the church how they propose that these will be delivered.

Most project managers are also quantity surveyors, which is very useful to the cost control process, as the same quantity surveyor can produce the budget to which the project runs. A project manager will offer a service including most of the following:

- Advice and assistance in appointing the consultants, the architect and other design team members, checking their contracts and agreeing fee levels to the advantage of the client.
- Assistance in preparing the client brief and project execution plan.
- Detailed programme for the project.
- Preparation of cost estimates, cost plans and cost-checking as the design is developed.
- Risk management, including managing contingency sums.
- Value management.
- Procurement and tendering the work.

- Contract documentation.
- Post-contract services including preparation of interim valuations, valuing any variations and agreeing the final account.[18]

As one project manager summarized, 'to ensure that the work can happen in a logical, economical and fundable order'. Putting the roles of project manager and quantity surveyor together in this way produces a good congruence between the management of the programme of works and cost.

The architect and the design team

The design and its delivery are the responsibility of the architect. The architect will meet with the church to be briefed on the scope of the works to be undertaken. The architect will review their own ability to complete the work, considering their own competence (for the type of work) and their commitments (can they work within the client's time frame?).

Negotiation will then take place with regard to the architect's terms of work. Though many churches forget this stage when working with their inspecting architect, it is essential that the prices are carefully considered. There are RIBA guidelines on the level of fee payments to architects, calculated as a percentage of the construction cost. This fee can be as high as 13.5% on a small but complicated piece of work. The percentage reduces with the increased cost of the works and with less complicated work. There will be tasks to do with building works that the architect cannot do and these will be taken on by several other essential professionals who become the design team to the project. The architect will then be the leader of the design team. See Notes on p. 112 on fee levels and their payment.

A surveyor may make accurate measurements and drawings of a new site or a building that is to be converted or refurbished, where no drawings currently exist. Today, this is often a computerized process that produces great accuracy very quickly, usually called a CAD survey.

---

18 Stuart Bremner, of Davis, Langdon & Everest, in a letter to a church in September 2000.

A quantity surveyor on all but small projects will first produce a budget estimate for the agreed design and will later produce a 'bill of quantities' for the tender stage. This ensures that builders submitting a tender are responding to a fully measured set of information that will enable accurate tender figures to be produced. The quantity surveyor will be the key person assessing the returned tenders to ensure that the lowest bidder has taken into account every aspect of the work and can be appointed. The quantity surveyor will attend site meetings (led by the architect) with the contractor and agree the actual valuations of work completed that normally happen on a monthly basis.

A structural engineer will be needed on the team for work that is structurally complex or significant.

The mechanical and electrical services engineer works on everything from drains and water supplies, heating and electrical services to air handling systems.

Other specialists may be appointed for archaeology, conservation, decorative work, joinery or other specialist work.

The client, the church, is responsible for all aspects of health and safety under the Construction (Design and Management) Regulations and to fulfil this obligation will ensure that a planning supervisor is appointed.

From the client's point of view each of these professionals will cost a percentage of the construction cost. Before agreeing anyone's fee it is important to build up a picture of what the total of all the roles will be and then ensure that the negotiated fees are not too high. Most projects should spend a maximum of 15% on fees. For extremely significant buildings, such as those listed Grade I, and where several different professionals are involved, this may rise to 18%. For a new building it will be the lower figure. So do not agree 11% for the architect and then discover that with three other professionals on board the percentage has to be reduced. Once fully agreed, these figures will be built into the contract between each design team member and the client. If you are doing a repair project partially funded by English Heritage and the Heritage Lottery Fund they will have set a maximum rate that they are prepared to contribute with grant aid.

The role of the project manager can be vital to keeping this and all other costs at a reasonable level. With help from the project manager the church appoints or confirms the professional team members, leaving the project manager to negotiate the fee levels (with an upper limit agreed with the church) with each of the team. Fees on a complicated project should not be agreed piecemeal. In a complicated project, for example with a large element of archaeology, the archaeology design specialist on the team will be paid a percentage fee against the archaeology element of the work. It is not necessary to pay the structural engineer working on the roof and beams a percentage of the whole work including the archaeology. The architect who will supervise everyone's work cannot expect to receive the same percentage from work that is designed by the structural engineer, but the architect's fee will reflect the fact that the architect is responsible for ensuring that the engineer's design is up to standard. Leave the complexities of this negotiation to the project manager. Once all fee levels and the scope of involvement has been agreed, each design team member will sign a contract with the church.

Note too that from the beginning of the project only one designated person from the church's side can give formal instruction (or even emergency instruction) to the project team. This avoids any confusion and the related added cost. If anyone speaks on behalf of the church council, he or she and the council must know that they have the authority to do so.

The Diocese of Southwark property department sent a letter in 1994 to all its churches about appointing architects and other professional advisers. It stipulated that the following matters should be agreed before any work is done. Their letter was a response to churches asking professional advisers to do pieces of work without ever having looked at what that design work was going to cost the church council:

1 Agree the extent of the work to undertaken, whether preliminary advice or formal recommendation. Before any further work or stage of work, a fresh written instruction must be prepared.
2 Agree the level of fees to be charged for each stage of the project and when those fees will be payable. The basis for the fees should be agreed in advance, including both the level and the time at which they are payable.
3 Agree on fees for abortive work. If the whole project does not go forward it is normal to pay those who have worked on it for their

time (a good reason for agreeing the fees for each stage as you go along and when you will pay them).[19]

4 Formal instructions. These should always be given in writing (except in clear emergencies), and when these come from the incumbent/vicar, it should be made clear that these are given on behalf of the church council and not by the vicar in his or her own right.

Summarize the brief from the church to the project design team

After all the church's discussions on the aims of the building project, prepare a summary. This, with good planning and design, will enable the building to meet all the church's objectives at the most economical price.[20]

The client's requirements:

• **User activities**. List all the possible activities the church plans to see undertaken in the building, along with the possible normal and maximum numbers of attendees and their frequency of attending the building. From this list, a schedule of room areas, finishes and storage requirements can be prepared. One room may cater for a number of different groups and activities over a week, so it is helpful to be as specific as possible by including the actual group times.

The easiest way to get started is with an 'Activity Schedule' with the following headings:

Activity; Average no. of attendees; Maximum no. of attendees; Time of activity; Special requirements; Location issues; Comments.

• **Special requirements**. Apart from any special requirements of particular user groups the summary should list the notes made by the church council with regard to design qualities: disabled access and provision, location, longevity and materials, general look of the building (modern,

---

19 Bear in mind too that the professional advisers will agree a fee level against an expected size of project financially. If that project then proves much cheaper than anticipated when the tenders are returned, there may be a problem for the advisers. RIBA has guidelines for resolving the subsequent negotiation. However, as has happened from time to time if the architect chooses themselves to design-in an additional piece of work in case there is enough money, and there proves not to be, then the fee level against the original agreed budget for the project applies.

20 Notes from Project Manager Iain Forrester of PRISM to a London church.

traditional), how rooms relate to one another, how people should be able to circulate, and services needed; and notes on other provision such as furniture storage, church office, refreshment facilities, outside tap for garden work, lighting frame for drama performances, and so on.

- **Layout**. Describe how you wish to run the building once it is in use, as the architect can then plan the best layout for ease of management. For example, having the church office by the main door can facilitate reception and supervision of use, but having it at the back can help its occupants get on with work uninterrupted. Consider how the premises will be staffed and supervised (see Chapter 15).

Initial design from the architect

Responding to the brief given by the church, the architect now comes up with a first idea for the layout and style of the building. The project manager/quantity surveyor can come up with a first draft indicative budget that will also inform the discussion about the design. Consider from every point of view how the design meets your objectives and in what ways it does not. As you imagine yourselves walking through and using the building, does it meet the needs or are some elements missing? Consider also the aesthetic ideas – Are they too detailed or fussy, are they attractive or necessary?

Does the building fit with your budget ideas or does it need to be simplified to be economically reasonable? This may mean changing your objectives as well as the design. Unless the church is funding all works out of its own resources – that is, it does not need funding from grantmakers – the total cost of works will need to be acceptable to outside funders, mainly that the church's chosen design is not an expensive way to build the facilities needed. For example, could a new community hall be built more economically from scratch than the cost being presented by the church for their adaptation?

If the design is fairly near to meeting the requirements, invite all church members to review the design and make comment. Have a meeting for local people so they too can comment. There may be excellent suggestions and ideas that help hone up the design.

After several meetings exchanging ideas and modifying the design, the architect will have worked the client's requirements into the final design. This will show the building's capacity, the layout, how the building will operate and the quality of the finishes. A more detailed indicative budget will then be prepared. This is also a good stage to begin to consult outside bodies for consents so that the design may still be adapted to accommodate their concerns.

The architect can then prepare drawings with the final design. The quantity surveyor prepares a Budget Estimate. The church council has a final review of the design and signs it off as acceptable or asks for final modification. The project manager will ensure that everyone has agreed and signed whatever formal agreements are needed. By this stage also the project manager will have ensured that the professional indemnity insurance of each member of the design team is in place and the insurers of the church have full details of what is planned; they may charge an additional sum over the normal payments.

Legal consents

Once the design has been accepted, the architect takes on the task of gaining all the necessary legal consents. Most churches are under faculty jurisdiction (see p. 52) and the design and necessary detail will be submitted to the Diocesan Advisory Committee and subsequently to the Diocesan Chancellor for permission to do the work. Planning permission will be required on external works, alteration or extension. If any change of use is involved, planning permission will also be required. Some local authorities require planning permission if there is a change of materials, for example from copper to slate on a roof: the architect should advise you on this.

For other buildings such as halls, or other additional building that is part of the church's investment plan, the whole project may come under planning permission not faculty jurisdiction or may need both, depending on the location, on whether the building or the land is consecrated and on whether it is in the church's curtilage. There are scores of other details that the architect will be required to comply with over aspects of the building, and most of these will be covered by building regulations, with local authority buildings regulations officers checking design details and visiting the site to ensure compliance.

Processing funds

The next stage of the process is like the parable of the man preparing to plough a field. It is time to check that the church is ready to go forward.

Check:

- Has the church got the money in the bank for going forward? The next steps of the process are very costly and once started on the building work there is no inexpensive way to turn back or go on hold!
- If money has still to be raised, do not start, but ask the architect to hold his further work while the church is fundraising. Do not start the building project till all the fundraising is complete *and* the money is in the bank.
- If grants are raised from major outside grantmaking trusts these will have contract terms with which the building project has to comply. For example, ensuring that the work goes out to tender to a minimum number of building companies.
- If money is raised from the Lottery Funds or from English Heritage a more complicated setup will be necessary for regular payments during the building phase. Set up the process before the work begins with a designated person to ensure every detail is correct. The project manager can oversee or undertake the management of this process.
- Ensure that the process is in place for the interim payment process that happens on the way through the building stage. Large sums of money may sensibly be held in a high interest account, so set up a process with the project manager to ensure that throughout the building programme that money is available to pay the builder's invoices promptly. The contract usually specifies payment within three weeks of invoice date.
- Ensure that everyone is clear about who is the church's key link person with the design team, so there are no abortive decisions; these would be very costly.
- Ensure that the church council knows when and how decisions will be brought to them during the process when details still need to be resolved. Start any decisions on paint colours and decorative finishes early as everyone will want to have their say and there must be no delay in providing information or again the delay will become expensive.

One impressive preliminary agreement between an architect and church project gave a very clear outline of the industry standards for when fees should be paid to the architect, and those for other professionals. The architect[21] gave a programme of when he would expect to invoice the church for fees and what proportion of his total fee that would represent.

Feasibility stage
Appraisal (the client has done this)
Strategic brief (hourly rate, rate given)

Pre-construction stage

Outline proposals	20%
Detailed proposals	20%
Final proposals	15%
Production information	20%
Tender documentation	2%
Tender Action	1%

Construction stage

Mobilization	1%
To practical completion	20%
After practical completion	1%

Following a process such as this, the church can note what proportion of the fees will be paid before the builders are on site (about 80%) and that invoices are submitted from when the architect starts work, in this case on a monthly basis. If the church has very little money for the development stage until fundraising is under way, it is possible to undertake fundraising with a quantity surveyor's indicative budget and outline drawings. The rest of the detailed work may be done when the funds have been raised so that the church has money available to pay the design team as the invoices are presented.

Detailed design and tendering

When all the money and processes are in place, the project begins to be designed in intricate detail. The architect's office will produce a large

---

21 Maxwell Hutchinson of Hutchinson Studio.

number of detailed drawings that show every aspect of the building works, down to the style of nuts and bolts. The quantity surveyor will work with these documents to produce a Bill of Quantities including the hours and costs of labour that will be required. Added in will be general building costs, scaffolding, security, health and safety provision and general labour. This gives the detailed cost of the design.

A meeting is then usually held between the client's link person (there may be others who attend this meeting also) and the design team. If it seems that with the detail designed that the work could exceed budget, decisions to alter details to get back to budget may be made. There are always items which can be amended, from the price of toilet fittings, to the style of floor tiles and the detail of electrical design that can be changed to bring the price back. The church does *not* have to accept increased cost; the only acceptable reason would be too long a delay between the accepted design and the decision to go ahead, during which time inflation may have taken up the overall cost of building works. The quantity surveyor can help look at this issue earlier in the process, adding in a greater contingency for inflation at the acceptance of the design stage.

The Bill of Quantities, in an unpriced format, and the design drawings, are sent out to a number of construction companies for each of them to tender for the contract. Often as many as five or six companies are approached, as not all will complete the process and the church will need at least three firm bids for selection.

At this point in the process, the members of the design team are due as much as 80% of their fees for the project. Fees are paid in stages throughout the project with a small amount only payable at Practical Completion.

All the tenders are returned by a specific date and time and opened *at the same time*. This ensures that there is no way that one tendering company can find out the content of another's bid and guarantee to undercut that bid. The quantity surveyor will check each bid in detail to spot mistakes or omissions and will bring back to the church and the design team a tender report. This will include a recommendation on which bid was actually the lowest taking into account every detail of the Bill that they have returned. The church will make a formal acceptance of the bid.

The Bill becomes the basis of a contract produced by the architect and the quantity surveyor. This is signed by the builder and the client. The project manager will ensure that the builder's insurance is fully in order and that they are financially able to take on the work. At this point the architect will see their role as primarily contract management, ensuring that the builders deliver the project to every detail contained in the contract. Design is complete, though there are always small details on which the builders and the architect will confer as the work proceeds.

On a monthly basis the design team will have a more formal meeting with the builders and the church's representative. Progress is reported, and problems reported although they are usually resolved outside of the meeting. Agreement is made on the *value of work completed to date*. This value is entered onto an Architect's Certificate and on the builder's invoice (which will include the VAT payable) and both will be sent to the church. Double check with the project manager before proceeding to pay these or any other invoices.

If major funders are involved they may wish to see the architect's certificate and the invoices before they are paid. This creates some pressure for paperwork to be dealt with without delay in order to ensure that builder's invoices are paid within the contracted period (usually three weeks). Normally this timescale is critical to the cashflow of the building company who are paying their staff and subcontractors every week. The church's undue delay in paying may result in the builder being forced into liquidation – it has happened – and the whole project being jeopardized. If the signatories to the church's bank account are likely to be away during the building process with a resultant delay in getting cheques signed, make alternative arrangements, such as adding new signatories to the account.

Regular conversation between the church and the architect and the project manager, both at the monthly site meeting and outside it, will often result in details of design being discussed. From the church's point of view, any change that the architect may identify as desirable or essential should be considered. The architect and the project manager should always tell the church representative of any cost implication to such issues, so if they do not, then ask. Just as the architect has to give written instruction to the contractor before any detailed change can be made, it is a good discipline for the church's representative to be under the same discipline; only written instructions and decisions are given to the architect by the client in order to keep costs down. No one other than the previously designated representative may give decisions from the church to the architect, and no one other than the architect can give instructions verbal or written to the builder. If a church member passes the site and is worried by what they see happening, they contact their representative, who in turn contacts the architect who then contacts the builder. This is cumbersome but is financially prudent.

Practical completion

Around the time of the work being complete, the architect will inspect the project in meticulous detail and produce a snagging list. The builder will then put all these usually small items right.

A certificate of Practical Completion is produced by the architect and final payments for the work are agreed. There will be retention of money, a small percentage of the total cost of the work, held by the client for one year.

The final payments to the architect and design team are now made.

Look out! Potential problems

Scaffolding. One of the first elements of refurbishment and repair to appear on site. Builders often leave a couple of weeks in their programme between scaffolding being erected and building workers coming to site. This allows for any delay by the scaffolding company (it is usually subcontracted to a specialist company) and prevents this impacting on the cost of workers being on site but unable to start.

Specifications. Any change in the specifications after the tender has been accepted will cost the client money. A good budget for the work will have included a contingency figure that covers unexpected problems or price rises but not be sufficient for either client or architect to change their minds as they go along. Careful discussions about design brief and specification and good project management will avoid this problem.

Client decisions/modifications. Expect to be charged for every modification and change, not just those that add work. A contract is binding even if less work is done, and any change that involves less work may only result in reduced cost *if the builder agrees*. For example, if the builder has already ordered and taken delivery of materials and cannot return them, or if the builder has contracts with other specialist companies, the client must pay.

Surprises. When a major refurbishment or repair project is under way, there will be talk of surprises, that is, items of work discovered only as the job proceeds. For example, when roof material is removed for refinishing, and it becomes apparent that the timbers beneath have rotted and need replacement. To avoid this and similar surprises, English Heritage/Heritage Lottery Fund grant-aided projects normally require some opening-up of roofs in a planning stage before the main works so the extent of the problem is more fully agreed. A well-prepared budget and a good development stage should anticipate such things, and on old buildings it is often advisable to have built in a higher contingency figure for just this reason.

Delays. If for any reason there is a delay during the building programme it will have a cost impact. One key task of the project manager will be to negotiate a final price with the builder that deals fairly with delays. The causes may include a client delaying a decision (colour of paint or tiles) or changing their mind (paint and tiles, furniture and fittings). The architect may be slow with detailed instruction; the builder may make a mistake in the programming (such as ordering late on materials that have an 8-week wait for delivery) and materials are not available on time. Something outside anyone's control may affect timing, a transport strike, or a mistake in supplying the stone. The project manager may well do some trade-offs to offset any delays caused by the client or the design team against any caused by the builder to keep the final price the same. But, for example, if wrongly supplied materials are not the builder's fault the costs of wasted time are passed on to the client.

Materials ordering and delivery time can affect price and it is worth at the design stage asking the architect to ensure that key items are readily available and a specialist material or fitting is not going to delay things when a small change in design could actually keep things on schedule.

Fixtures and fittings proving very expensive. There are multitudes of designs of light fittings, taps and toilets that can be fitted in the facilities a church needs. When the cost of fancy taps is multiplied by the total number needed it can prove a big item on the budget. Consider asking the architect to recommend taps, door handles, locks, sinks, toilets, lights and other fittings that are functional and sturdy but inexpensive. Check that local suppliers are available for specialist light fittings and that all lights will be easily accessible for bulb changes.

Change of value. If fundraising has taken a long time then the prices may have risen from those first indicated by the quantity surveyor. However, the tender prices should reflect the actual cost of fairly immediate work. *At the time of the tender report*, before the contract is signed, get the project manager to negotiate dropping some items, or reduce the cost of some items if it looks as though the project is over budget.

Cashflow problems. Once the builders are on site they will invoice at monthly intervals and will be entitled to be paid for all work completed in the previous month. Payment is normally contracted to be made within three weeks of invoice date. The quantity surveyor will prepare a cashflow projection for the duration of the project that enables the church to know when amounts of money are expected to be needed. A client should never have builders working on something for which the complete funding is not available. Use the cashflow projection as a guideline for drawing money from a savings account to the current account, not as a guide for fundraising. The funds promised by outside funders should be in the bank before you start.

How to mitigate the things that go wrong or may go wrong. The design team, especially the project manager, should produce a risk analysis for the project from the professional side and should set in place the best possible mitigation and contingency provision in face of pitfalls.

However, it is extremely constructive for the church to undertake a risk analysis for all the things that are under its power and its responsibility. To create a chart as in Figure 14.2, maybe for a discussion at the church council meeting, and to fill in the mitigating actions, can be very fruitful. Often the fears that make some members vote against the project are worthwhile concerns that should be addressed and mitigating action determined. In the early planning stages a good question could be, 'What if there really aren't any people out there who want to book our hall, it will be a complete waste of money and effort?' The risk analysis suggests considering the impact of this scenario happening and what we can do to ensure it does not. For example, a thorough audit of local facilities and enquiries for space will indicate whether the parish needs more facilities. Equally, a good public relations programme once the facilities are complete will ensure that people know they are now available for booking. Such mitigation only works if it is followed through in an action plan.

Insurance. The church's insurance company should be fully apprised of the building work that is to happen. They may ask for an additional premium and will expect the project manager to ensure that all the professional indemnities and builder's insurance are in place.

Construction (Design and Management). The health and safety of all workers on site, the general public and the people who use the building once the work is complete are protected by legislation. Health and safety are the responsibility of the client, in this case the church, who discharges that responsibility before and during the building programme through the appointment of a planning supervisor. This will cost between 0.5% and 1% in the fee structure. At the end of the building works, the planning supervisor gives the client a report on what's fitted and guidelines for its safe use.

Professional indemnity. Members of the design team are covered by professional indemnity insurance for what they design on the building, and its failure or inappropriateness for the building. It's not often called on but can be dramatic when it does happen: wrongly designed church foundations, or even the Millennium Bridge that wobbled. The indemnity is needed for such rare occasions. The project manager will ensure the level of professional indemnity is high enough to cover the church's project.

Figure 14.2 Risk Assessment for the Project Strategy

Risk	Probability of Occurrence	Impact of Occurrence	Mitigating Planning and Action
Failure of Maintenance programmes	The building has not had a challenging maintenance programme in the past, so managing an effective programme is new and significant. Low probability of problems.	Failure of maintenance contracts on the lift and similar critical facilities could have immediate effect on the licensed status. High impact on financial plans. Failure of routine maintenance on minor items, redecoration and similar items will reduce lettability. Medium and increasing impact on financial viability	Maintenance is a key element in the financial and facilities management that has resulted in the present strategy for viability. Within the Church Council, there are people with the skills to ensure the establishment of a programme that fulfils the work of the Ten-Year Maintenance Plan. The Church Council will address maintenance through regular reports from the administrator and churchwardens on maintenance and repair programmes; reports and spot checks on facilities will be undertaken; reports on standards of similar premises will inform upgrading in future years. Financial Planning now includes adequate funds to maintain and repair the building.

continued

Risk	Probability of Occurrence	Impact of Occurrence	Mitigating Planning and Action
Failure of Repair programmes	The building has had no major repairs in recent decades. Quinquennial repairs are not expected to be major in the near future, but regular repair will be needed. This will include items from the Ten-Year Plan, plus items identified in Quinquennial reports. Over the next fifty years major works will be needed to high levels and this is inevitable. Low probability of occurrence.	Quinquennial repairs in the medium term are not expected to have high impact. Long term: some repairs will have high impact eventually with a high cost.	It is crucial that long-term planning prepares for both minor and major repairs. This is a critical element of the financial planning and the establishment of a Sinking Fund for repairs is planned from the outset. An annual review of designated and restricted repair funds will be undertaken to affirm that the accrual of funds is adequate for future works as far as can be anticipated.

| Loss of key staff | The management of high quality facilities, with high level of use in a Grade I building requires staff with considerable relevant experience and commitment, both volunteer and paid staff.

Loss of such staff once in post is of low probability in the immediate future. | Medium impact. | The Church Council takes full responsibility for the overall strategy and will develop more detailed contingency including making plans for staff holidays, illness, absence and loss. This will allow for the shortest possible break in service or interruption in programmes.

Plans will be made for any interregnum between clergy to have minimum possible impact on the building, its programmes and its maintenance. |
| Failure of security and safety of staff and public | Given the location and being open every day, St Jude's Church will need continuing vigilance over security and safety.

All staff are at risk from verbal and physical attack (statistics of the Diocese of London).

Medium probability. | Medium impact if comprehensive policies and procedures are operated and all staff are well trained. | Ongoing staff training in practical aspects of alarms, fire and all other hazards. Training on dealing with all visitors. Training on dealing with difficult and abusive members of the public. Training on dealing with emergencies and in First Aid. |

continued

Risk	Probability of Occurrence	Impact of Occurrence	Mitigating Planning and Action
Failure of income	Failure or loss of targeted additional sources of income from outside groups. Arts and community groups and commercial office letting. Inevitable changes in day-to-day lettings. Medium probability.	High impact.	Early establishment of marketing programme to find suitable users and tenants before works are complete. Regular monitoring of letting frequency to facilitate tackling problems early. Contingency planning to be undertaken to allow for financial accrual to cover voids and for quickly finding new tenants and partner projects.
Excess of expenditure over income	There are a number of unchanging overheads such as insurance and staff costs that will be expended regardless of fluctuating programmes. Others such as lighting will be less if the programme reduces. The possibility of expenditure exceeding income is a high probability.	High impact.	Immediate action required to identify or raise working capital to create viable cashflow from day one of re-opening. Vigilance through the staff producing monthly reports on finance so that problems are anticipated and dealt with quickly by the Church Council. Development of contingency fund that is able to cover ups and downs in cashflow.

| Loss of commercial tenant | Medium probability. | Low impact. | To minimize the impact of a tenancy change, the church will secure a rent deposit from incoming tenants and have contingency plans ready for action as soon as a tenant gives notice to quit. |
| Loss or failure of Community Project/Arts Project tenant | Low probability. | Medium impact. | The church will ensure that all agreements are thoroughly established on a professional basis so that clear decision making processes are in place. While the rental level is appropriate to a community project, in all other ways this will be managed in exactly the same way as the commercial lease.

Contingency plans will be set. |

Snagging. This refers to a detailed list compiled by the architect of all the mostly minor work that is incomplete, has been missed or is not up to standard when the project is drawing to a close. If the client notices any problems these must be pointed out as soon as possible. If these items are incomplete when the builders leave the site they will often remain incomplete, so the architect will be nagging the builder about them for the last part of the contract time on site.

15

Managing People and Buildings

A church that is moving from being staffed by one clergy person and occasional volunteers to everyday opening with lettings to other groups and organizations will almost undoubtedly have to employ additional staff. The purpose of this section is to highlight areas that a good employer will address. If those in key roles in the church have little or no experience in employment practice or managing personnel, then resources and references suggest places to go for more detailed preparation. The Church Urban Fund has produced an excellent handbook on employment practice, and the Directory of Social Change runs excellent seminars and publishes a number of books on employment practice. It is not the purpose of this book to be a handbook, for example, on the intricacies of PAYE or the employer's responsibilities for National Insurance. These are well presented in other places.[22] It is our purpose to highlight some key issues in employing people in the management of church buildings.

New uses

Assuming that the church is beginning to set up an everyday programme for opening, a good starting-point is to list all the tasks that need to be done, daily or weekly, and to what standard. Then in a third column indicate whether someone already does this task in some way. This will facilitate both the assessment of the work to be done, preparing job descriptions of new posts and undertaking proper reviews as the programme goes forward.

---

22 There are a number of books in the catalogue of the Directory of Social Change that will help with the detail of each of these issues.

Task	Frequency and standard	Whose job?
Unlocking church or hall and locking up at the end of the day	Monday to Saturday	Currently clergy; can their availability increase with new uses?
Setting up: lights, visitor guides, heating and other requisites	Daily	Currently clergy; can their availability increase with new uses?
Writing visitor guides	Occasional	Volunteers
Cleaning toilets and kitchen	Daily	Currently volunteers on Saturdays; can they cover every day?
Watching: for visitors with needs and for security		Currently volunteers on Saturdays; can this increase?
Caring for visitors with pastoral needs	May drop in at any time	Clergy currently make appointments. Who will cope with everyday drop-ins?
Daily offices		Clergy
Repairs: minor and major		Currently the churchwardens; can they cope with the increase with new uses?
Booking maintenance visits for lift, fire protection, boiler and other contracts	Annual and at emergencies	Currently the churchwardens; can they cope with the increase with new uses?
Taking bookings by groups and individuals	Daily intermittent	New: administrator

Task	Frequency and standard	Whose job?
Running the diary, ensuring key holders available and that deposits are made and returned	Daily but must be accurate and systematic to avoid mishaps	New: administrator
Book-keeping	High standard needed	New: part-time book-keeper
Building: letters and phone calls		New: administrator
Reception		New
Newsletter and updates for all who regularly use the church		New
Advertising the space available		New
Closing up, switching off lights, lowering heat, checking all areas are empty and secure, setting alarms		Currently clergy and the churchwardens. Does this need to be covered by a caretaker?
First Aid	Occasional	New: Arrange training for staff and volunteers

This list is not exhaustive: have a brainstorming session to add the elements that are required for your church's premises.

Leadership

The leader holds together the vision and strategy and ensures these are carried through into the activity of the organization. In a church leadership includes clergy, churchwardens and members of the church council. The leader motivates others through their own commitment and example. They encourage, affirm and advise as they participate.

A team can function as a co-operative and mutually supportive group with a common purpose or can equally end up as a series of independent people each following their own job description with no sense of common purpose. Drawing people together requires collective activity.

To build a constructive co-operative team,

- Ensure that everyone is familiar with the church's purposes, aims and values and has had opportunity for each person to voice the way these fit into their work tasks.
- Work together on the annual objectives so that everyone is party to and committed to the targets for the year, especially any changes or new tasks.
- Ensure that there are team rules that everyone has agreed together. These can include giving everyone opportunity to speak and be listened to; exercising respect in talking about each other, present or not; listening and asking questions before jumping to conclusions; being honest with one another, including about feelings, slights and grudges; being courteous to one another, especially when there are disagreements. Members of the team can then keep each other to the agreed rules.

Regular staff meetings

Start each meeting with reports from staff on how their work is going and how they are feeling about their work. Encourage listening and considering creative solutions where things are not going well. Team members who understand each other and each other's work can support and encourage one another, or act as a sounding board as problems arise.

Problems are often opportunities to do something new or different. Some team members may be good at devising new solutions. However, if one person comes with a problem from their work area it may be helpful for the team members to make suggestions but *leave the individual worker or the worker with their line manager* to decide which if any of these solutions might be used.

Ensure that people whose job involves repetitive tasks, such as cleaning, are not treated as personally any less significant, nor their job as less significant, than others. Similarly people who have few problems with their work should have as much time being listened-to as those who raise problems. For a big staff group, workers may take turns at talking about their work at successive meetings.

Motivating the team to look forward optimistically is a challenge for those with leadership roles. The leader does not have to have all the answers and it is far better if they do not suggest their own answers too quickly, even if they have ideas. Team members will develop much more fully as workers and people if they find and enact their own solutions. When a problem is presented the leader can ask open-ended questions:

'Do you have any ideas of how this might be solved?'

'Does anyone else have ideas or experience that might help __?'

'Do any of these suggestions seem helpful?'

'Does anyone else see preferred solutions?'

Only if the problem arising is not within the realm of that person's work should the leader even appear to take over the problem. For example, the cleaner complains about people walking on the freshly washed and wet floor making it immediately a mess again. Asked for possible solutions, the cleaner simply wants to stop people doing it. Another worker suggests one solution could be to buy a couple of 'slippery wet floor' signs from a supply catalogue, as it's not just an issue of mess but of hazard to people who walk there. All the leader has needed to do is ask the questions.

Areas of common concern – staff safety, breaches in health and safety policies, budgetary issues and others – can be approached with the same openness and produce suggestions of solutions and ways forward that keep to the ground rules of the team. If it becomes clear that a particular member of staff is repeatedly failing to keep to an agreed principle, for example over security or safety, this should be resolved with their line manager away from the group. Similarly for any staff grievance.

Annually the church council will set a new budget, which will impact on the staff and their work areas. Staff may prepare a draft budget individually, work over it as a team and then give this to the budget-setting committee with the reasons for any changes, increase or decrease, on previous years. The team leader can then bring back the budget as set and discuss how the staff can work within it. It is a way for a staff team to work to fulfil the strategy and aims of the organization's leaders, thereby working out the management aspects of mission.

There are many issues in a church that can affirm teamwork or isolate members from each other. Clergy work with complex issues that could result in them not being as open with the team as is helpful for team development. A one-way sharing is no sharing. There are many aspects of a priest's work that church members and staff understand intuitively, such as the confidentiality of the pastoral work, or the rather chaotic nature of a schedule that may be interrupted at any moment by a pastoral crisis, or the need to have quiet times of preparation for services. When the priest explains these issues to the team then the team becomes their support group also. For example, the priest may simply say 'Here's when I am taking holiday this year,' expecting everyone else to fit around this, or they may say, 'Here's the family and pastoral issues that control when I can take my holiday, so I would prefer ___.' In a team that has established mutual respect, the priest will still get the holiday at the best time.

In a more autocratic world of previous generations in the Church, clergy were the bosses rather than team leaders. With many clergy receiving no training on how to work co-operatively with a team, the old pattern persists as the only known way to work. Talking about ways to change is critical to new patterns of staff teamwork.

Not everyone needs to know everything that is happening, but most people like to know as much as possible. A staff communication strategy should be set up. The staff meeting can be the key place and so all staff should be present even when their part of the work schedule is minor.

Display schedules that show who is doing what, who will be in on what dates and what groups are using the church when. Greater openness and more information along with a creative atmosphere will enable people to pull together to make things work even when problems arise or misunderstandings cause difficulty. However, there are occasionally people who are obsessive about 'not knowing' what is going on. In reality they may know all that it is reasonable to know, but are suspicious or insecure – deal with this as a pastoral issue.

Decisions

On a small church staff team it can be important to consider the way that decisions are made. Is responsibility shared or delegated by the leader or manager? People who are included in responsibility often work harder and more effectively than otherwise.

The team leader may consult everyone on significant decisions that in any way affect their work or the workplace. Consult means hearing everyone's input before making a decision.

Consensus decisions are those on which a whole group comes to common agreement. Decisions that affect everyone's working life but are not very relevant outside the staff circle are best done by consensus, for example, holiday rotas, breaks during the day, details for the staff Christmas dinner and so on.

Decisions made by the church council outside of the church staff group should, where these impact on the staff, be communicated to the staff at the earliest opportunity. It impacts negatively on morale if staff hear information that affects their work on the grapevine or in general chatter after church on Sunday. If church council decisions impact on an individual's contracted work, then that individual must agree before the change can be implemented.

Outline structure

Every worker should know to whom they are accountable for their work. When a management group meets regularly its first key task should be to receive a report from one or more workers. With a larger team individuals may report monthly to their line manager. Only one person in the organization should be able to discuss any disciplinary issue with any worker, that is, their line manager. The same person will meet with their worker annually for appraisal. It is a relationship that works best in an atmosphere of mutual respect. If respect is lost or mistrust becomes evident on either side it is time for serious review with outside help.

Job descriptions

Every worker should have their own job description as agreed with their manager. Changes should be by mutual agreement. Normally the job description is drawn up before a person is employed and is the basis of the work contract. When there is no job description (and this a common problem in churches) then neither worker nor manager really knows what the worker should be doing or when, and irritation often grows as the unspoken expectations of each begin to cause problems.

Volunteers who work regularly should also have job descriptions, perhaps written by themselves so they are really saying what they are prepared to offer of time and skills. They should also know what to do if a problem arises.

Clergy do not have job descriptions for themselves and are not apparently in a line of accountability except in dire circumstances. Therefore they often ignore the lack of good procedure with their own staff. Many difficult staff relationship problems in churches could be avoided if staff have proper job descriptions and regular appraisal, and good practice in management of staff is developed.

People

Many busy and effective churches are run by a small army of volunteers. It is never good to assume that already busy people will not be available to help. Because they love their church and are committed to its future they will make the effort and fit in more hours. It is preferable to give people the opportunity to contribute. (Be careful not to overburden willing volunteers, with the result that they give up!)

When there really are no volunteers available (and some churches are unable to find more than one or two) then it is time to consider employing people for key tasks.

Set out the hours required for new tasks to be completed. Against these (as above) put in the names of volunteers and highlight the tasks for which no one is able to offer time and skills. Identify the skills and the times in drawing up a job description and hours to be worked. The appropriate salary can be set by looking at such work as it is advertised in your local paper.

An assessment of how the cost of new staff will be met out of income from new activity in the church is expressed in a budget and cashflow projection.

The following is an example of key duties of an Administrator, to be adapted for the specific situation in your church.

Duties of the administrator

General
- To manage and administrate the use of the Church Hall Committee (Parochial Church Council) along guidelines agreed with the Chair of the Committee.
- To promote access and use of the Church Hall (Church) to the local community, the borough and to the general public.
- To implement the policies of the Church Hall Committee (Parochial Church Council) with regard to the use of the premises.
- To be responsible to the Committee Chair for the following specific duties.

Specific
- To ensure day-to-day financial administration in consultation with the Treasurer and book-keeper, including: payment of invoices, banking, maintaining cashbooks and balances, reconciliation of bank statement, salary payments, raising invoices and chasing unpaid invoices, maintaining petty cash imprest system.
- To develop and co-ordinate bookings and lettings by different users of the church with regular and occasional users.
- To service the meetings of the Church Hall Committee/Parochial Church Council including attendance at meetings.
- To develop increasing use by the local community; include developing promotional leaflets, information packs, educational and other relevant material.

- To supervise staff: administration, cleaners, and caretaker.
- To ensure through clearly structured and presented guidelines that all visitors respect the use of the building as a worshipping church/church hall.
- To co-ordinate maintenance of the building in agreement with the Chair of the Church Hall Committee/Parochial Church Council and to liaise with maintenance and repair contractors.
- To work with the Chair of the Church Hall Committee/Parochial Church Council to continue the restoration of the building.
- To meet regularly with the Chair of the Church Hall Committee/Parochial Church Council.
- To undertake other duties as agreed with the Chair of the Church Hall Committee/Parochial Church Council.

The following is an example of key duties of a Caretaker, to be adapted for the specific situation in your church.

Duties of the caretaker

General
- To be the main key holder for out-of-hours lettings of the Church Hall.
- To undertake minor maintenance and repair tasks as agreed with the Committee.
- To be on duty to provide care of the premises during agreed hours while the building is in use.
- The job will involve evening and weekend working.

Specific
- To agree with the Administrator the specific hours of work on a weekly basis.
- To provide on-site emergency cleaning and minor repair duties as agreed with the Administrator.
- To call out emergency repair contractors as agreed with the Administrator.
- To provide low-key supervision of the building and its users while on duty, ensuring policies such as health and safety and guidelines of the Church Hall Committee are maintained.
- To undertake other duties as agreed with the Administrator.

Ensure also that the responsibilities of the line manager are clearly defined.

The working environment

People aren't machines – caring for their welfare means providing a good working environment, in the midst of busy programmes and schedules. It is worth taking time to consider each worker and the place in which their job is located. Is that environment encouraging and affirming, can they take pride in their job, are they affirmed in the part they play in the whole, does each person have someone they can easily talk to about aspects of work that are inadequate or unhelpful? Not just in theory but in practice?

Consider:
- Pleasant surroundings.
- Available daylight and quality of electrical light.
- Cleanliness and absence of clutter.
- Privacy when it is needed.
- Toilets that are clean and attractive.
- Place for refreshments and relaxation for tea breaks, not just at the worker's desk.
- Adequate equipment that is safety checked.
- Properly laid out desks spaces for those working on computers.
- Full assessment of health and safety at work.

Responsibilities of being an employer

Every employer has legal and moral responsibilities for the staff they employ, and churches are not an exception. Most responsibilities are a matter of law.

Contract. Every employee should be given a contract within six weeks of beginning work. The key elements of a contract of employment are listed in Appendix 4. The absence of a contract does not leave the employee unprotected, as the law deems a contract to be in place after six weeks, its key elements being considered those that have been practised while the employee has been there, along with all the basic working rights that the law requires, from holiday and sick pay to working hours and rate of pay. If there is any reason for the church to wish to have special elements included such as no overtime pay but rather time-off-in-lieu, then a contract signed by both parties is the proper way.

Equal Opportunities

Churches are, like every organization, subject to the law on discrimination. Regardless of whether or not the church writes an Equal Opportunities statement it is obliged to comply with the law. With a few exceptions for fundamental aspects of belief, it is not permitted to discriminate against people on a number of grounds including gender, race, sexual orientation or religion. With the traditions of the church, problems may arise.

Staff can be recruited on the basis of their religion or belief where this is a genuine occupational requirement of the job.[23] This is only applicable when a 'job holder needs to practise a specific religion in order to undertake the role within the ethos of the organization'. 'Organisations can reasonably expect their staff to keep their organizational values and culture and should bear in mind that people may be able to maintain those values and culture without actually belonging to the particular religion or belief.' If there were to be an Employment Tribunal claim that an organization is discriminating against someone on the grounds of religion, 'then the burden of proof will be on the employer to show there is a genuine occupational requirement'.

For an organization to claim that a particular religious belief is necessary, the first step is to analyse the duties of a worker and for each of these duties to show that any particular religious duty could not be undertaken by another member of staff. Clearly the employment of a priest, vicar or minister is an exception, as the majority of the role requires the jobholder to undertake specifically religious duties most of the time. If the jobholder duties are management, administration, caretaking or cleaning there is unlikely to be a significant element of the job that requires them to perform a religious duty. If the manager would normally start a meeting with a prayer, clearly another person could fulfil that task. Similarly if having a non-Christian on the staff would not significantly impact on the profile of the organization, an exception will not be made. Remember, the burden of proof that an exception is necessary is on the employer.

---

23 A booklet explaining the law on religion and Equal Opportunity can be downloaded (as can all their booklets) from the ACAS website at www.acas.org.uk or is obtainable by phoning the helpline on 08457 47 47 47.

Recruiting with Equal Opportunities

Prepare a job description outlining all the tasks to be undertaken and make clear which skills are essential to the post and which are merely desirable. Ensure you do not add criteria that would discourage applicants because of their religion or belief. Similarly, ensure that as the recruitment process continues that selection is made based on the skills and aptitude for the job. Avoid raising personal issues that are not about how well the person can do the job. This includes avoiding questions about marital status or childcare responsibilities or in any way implies potential discrimination on such grounds.

The short-listing panel and the interviewing panel should be the same person or people, and each applicant should be asked the same questions set around the areas of skill required. Clarifying details may be asked for to allow a candidate to answer more fully.

The order in which candidates present themselves can affect their chances of getting the job, even when their abilities are similar, unless the interviewing panel operates in an egalitarian way. It is helpful to find a method (such as points out of 5) of grading each person's response to each question as the interview proceeds, so that their ability is not overlooked simply because three more candidates follow. Take brief notes so that after the interviews as the selection panel discusses the candidates you can call to mind every person's responses. Add to this process several other smaller but critical issues. Make the decision only on the basis of the interviews, not on prior knowledge of a candidate nor with information or opinion from someone who is not an interviewer. The interview panel makes the decision to be ratified by the church council.

Create a table. Agree the content of each question, clearly relating to the job description. Each panel member completes their own copy of the table.

This enables every candidate to be asked the same questions and their performance remembered by the panel even after several people have been interviewed. Time should be allowed between candidates for the panel to make any additional notes.

These forms and all notes made by members of the panel should be retained, as any particular candidate may wish to find out why they did not get the job and to ensure that they were treated fairly. It is the

Name of Candidate			
Agreed question (prepared by panel around essential activity in job description)	Panel member to ask question	Key elements needed in answer	Candidate's score out of 5
1			
2			
3			
4			
5			

evidence that may be used if there is any tribunal or legal action taken against the employer.

PAYE

Setting up or running a PAYE system, to ensure that appropriate tax and national insurance are paid, can be undertaken by the church treasurer. Some dioceses are prepared to add local church employees to the diocesan payroll, undertaking the administration of the system and receiving monthly direct debit payments from the parish for the salary itself.

There are still churches or clergy that find themselves persuaded into paying 'cash in hand'. There are almost no circumstances where this is acceptable legally. If any payment is repeated then an employment agreement is implied, therefore this is subject to employment law. The employer is obliged to ensure that employer's National Insurance is paid, and unless the employee can produce evidence of exemption, should deduct the employee's National Insurance and Income Tax. A casual one-off afternoon of gardening may be acceptable for cash in hand, but a regular cleaner or caretaker must be set up for PAYE.

People living on Supplementary Benefit often present a very plausible case, when working just a few hours each week, for keeping the whole process quiet. However, if 'found out' the employee will have to refund the Supplementary Benefit they have received while working and the employer, the church, will have to pay all the back-dated National Insurance. Only a regular situation of employment should be entered into.

Staff welfare

Toilets and rest space

Staff who work in stressful or busy environments need a rest room where they can switch off from the pressure during their break, and get away from the phone and the other demands for their attention. It is not helpful for staff to take their coffee and lunch breaks at their desks. Even the addition of an easy chair can be helpful where space is limited.

The staff toilet should be clean and presentable. Many church toilets are substandard and the refurbishment of toilet cubicles can be inexpensive and readily achieved.

Support

Many clergy choose or accept very pressurized work environments and it is very easy for it to become an expectation that church staff accept the same pressures. But not everyone can work well under pressure and many tasks cannot be achieved with difficult deadlines, constant interruptions and chaotic administration.

Identify the desired working context that will enable each staff member to do their best in their work and support the staff in maintaining this. For example, don't remove stationery items from the administrator's desk or move papers around. Respect one another's filing systems. Agree on access to the cleaning materials and equipment so the cleaner does not always have to hunt down equipment before starting work. Have a system so that staff on their lunch breaks are not continuing to answer the phone.

All staff should be able to expect the loyalty and respect of their fellow workers.

Computer workstation

Most church administrators spend most of the day at a workstation. I have seen administrators trying to cope with a workstation set up for the vicar that does not allow the layout or chair height to be altered; this is a health and safety hazard for the administrator, and staff should not be squashed into uncomfortable corners that are designed for 'making do' but not for regular work.

Every worker should have a computer station set up for their own comfort and safety. If more than one person will use the computer in the course of the day/week then each must be able to adjust it to their own needs. Check the following details:

- The monitor should be 50–75 cm from the eyes with the top of the screen at or below eye level. The head and neck should be forward and upright, not bent or turned.
- Feet should be flat on the floor or on a footrest.
- The chair must offer support to the lower back and have adequate padding for personal comfort.
- There should be 5 cm clearance between the back of the knees and the chair seat.
- The keyboard should be 2.5 cm above the level of the elbows, and hands and wrist using the keyboard should be in a straight line, with no awkward bend up or down. Adding a mouse mat with built-in wrist-rest may be helpful.
- Source documents should be held as nearly as possible in line with the screen, to reduce head movement and neck strain. Use a document holder attached to the side of the screen.
- The space under the desk should be clear to allow leg-room and room to stretch.
- The location of the computer in relation to windows and overhead lights may produce glare. If the computer is against the window the light contrast may be a problem too. An anti-glare screen may help solve the problem.[24]

---

24 From 3M Innovation.

Supervision

Staff supervision involves setting realistic and agreed targets and standards for each member of staff that are very specific to their particular job. When staff member and supervisor do not agree tasks and the quality with which they are completed, the unspoken expectations are often unrealistic and the cause of breakdown in relationships. When agreed targets are not met, constructive feedback and review will root out the causes and address the problems.

Most people who are not doing well are aware of the problems. Though the language may be more complicated and more specific, a good review will ask the staff member what they think is going well in their job, what areas they would like to improve, and what training they would like to undertake to improve their skills. Additionally most good employers like to encourage (and some pay for) training and development that is not directly related to the job to increase the morale and overall skill set of employees, thus looking after personal development targets.

Dealing with conflict

From time to time there will be conflict between staff members. It is important to listen to both parties *before* drawing any kind of conclusion. After hearing both, bring them together with a view to finding a way forward that is –if not amicable – at least workable.

Ongoing conflict that is about working practice should be resolved by a committee decision on good practice. Personal problems that affect work relationships should be dealt with confidentially with the line manager.

Set up a strategy for dealing with conflict between a staff member and their manager that acknowledges the need at times for third-party help. If a staff member is line managed by the chair of the committee, who is also the vicar, this gets very complicated. But in order to avoid legal action or an employment tribunal that is both expensive and divisive, set up another person to whom the staff member may go if a problem arises. This may be another member of the committee or a skilled outsider.

It is advisable, for good practice, for an employer to have the ACAS booklet on grievance and disciplinary procedures, *Discipline at Work*, referring to the booklet in staff contracts as the way such issues will be addressed.

Dismissal

Proper procedures must be used in dismissing staff, or the employer may find that legal action is taken. Again *Discipline at Work*, free from ACAS, outlines proper procedure and the acceptable reasons and ways that an employee may be dismissed. Absenteeism and being late, long-term sickness and other poor patterns of attendance are subjects for disciplinary procedure after proper discussion with the employee in endeavouring to solve problems. These issues are only a cause for dismissal after the appropriate disciplinary procedure has been followed. Harassment between members of staff is a subject for disciplinary procedures, leading to dismissal if behaviour is persistent.

Redundancy

Making an employee redundant is appropriate when the job they are doing is going to cease to exist because of organizational change or lack of money to pay for it. A person is not redundant if the job will be re-established after they have gone.

Maternity leave is a provision that every employer must make. The possibility of maternity leave is not acceptable legal grounds for not employing a woman.

HIV Aids is not an acceptable cause for failing to select someone at interview or for dismissing a staff member. There are very effective health and safety practices that may be put in place to ensure that safety is maintained.

Common abuses in the church workplace

Bullying is common in churches and charities and usually the result of very poor employment practice. The bully is often an out-of-their-depth senior staff member who has failed to set proper agreements on tasks and work quality with those they manage. When the employee is more skilled in an area than their manager, the manager may feel inadequate and defensive, resulting in offensive behaviour. Resentment, personal inadequacy, personality clashes, unwarranted criticism, indiscretion, gossip, secretiveness can all result in bullying behaviour. Bullying happens very commonly between vicars and their assistant curates. The solution is proper training of all staff for their roles and good practice in managing others.

Overwork is common in churches. It becomes counterproductive, as tired workers are not enthusiastic, motivated or creative in their work. They may sink into negativity about themselves and others and become incrementally less effective and efficient at their work. Except in unusual circumstances and occasionally, each worker should only be working the hours agreed in their contract. Clergy have neither agreed hours nor regular work hours but when they line manage other staff it is extremely important that a good employment pattern is set up.

Security of staff at work is the employer's responsibility. In London, research has shown that clergy are more likely to be attacked at work than most other working groups, coming third behind police and prison officers – higher than social workers or teachers. Dioceses are trying to address this problem for their clergy and to make sense of safety in churches, but every individual church is responsible for the safety of its workers, volunteers and visitors. The staff team should discuss processes and guidelines for ensuring staff safety at work, especially when dealing with visitors and the general public. Many disoriented, drunk or drugged people head for the church to seek a place of refuge, but may not take No for the answer when they make demands. A worker alone in a building that is open to the public is especially vulnerable. Each staff member must have agreed and effective ways to get help, as it is needed. Personal alarms or other facilities should be available and readily accessible. When staff leave the workplace for meetings or visits they should always tell someone where they are going or leave a record of their destination on their desks, so that if there is an incident they may be traced or contacted.

Appendix 1

Risk Analysis Chart

Use a chart such as the one below to list your own church's specific risks and plan for mitigating action, giving special attention to those risks that would have a high impact on the church's life and ministry

Risk	Likelihood of happening (low, medium, high)	Impact of happening (low, medium, high)	Mitigating action that will be undertaken now

Appendix 2

Chart for Schedule and Brief Preparation

One church's assessment of the facilities they need in preparation for a brief for the architect. It tells the architect the functions needed but not how to design the building.

Activity	Current location	Average numbers	Maximum numbers	Time	Special requirements	Location issues	Comments
Sunday							
Children's parties	L H	50	50	pm			Refreshments preparation
Children's parties	S H	25	25	pm			Refreshments preparation
Sunday School	S H	4	10	am			
After church refreshments		50	70	am			Additional to present hall use
Monday							
Kidsworks	L H	30	30	am			Refreshments preparation
Luncheon club (new)		20	25	Noon +pm		kitchen	Additional to present hall use
Table tennis	L H	10	15	eve			
Playgroup	S H	30	30	am			Refreshments preparation
Beavers	S H	24	30	eve			
Scouts	S H	30	30	eve			

L H = Large Hall   S H = Small Hall

continued

Activity	Current location	Average numbers	Maximum numbers	Time	Special requirements	Location issues	Comments
Tuesday							
Aerobics	L H	120	50	am			Refreshments preparation Come & go during am
Table tennis	L H	10	15	eve			
Social group	S H	25	30	am			
Elderly fellowship	S H	12	15	eve			
Wednesday							
Aerobics	L H	120	50	am			Refreshments preparation Come & go during am
Luncheon club (new)		20	25	Noon +pm		kitchen	Additional to present hall use
Bingo (elderly)	L H	35	40	eve			Refreshments preparation
P. & toddlers	S H	20	25	am			Refreshments preparation
Venture Scouts	S H	20	25	eve			
Thursday							
Kidsworks	L H	30	30	am			Refreshments preparation
Tai chi	L H	25	30	eve			
Playgroup	S H	30	30	am			Refreshments preparation
Cubs	S H	35	40	eve			

Friday							
Aerobics	L H	120	50	am			Refreshments preparation Come & go during am
Luncheon club (new)		20	25	Noon +pm		kitchen	Additional to present hall use
Martial arts	L H	25	30	eve			
Playgroup	S H	30	30	am			Refreshments preparation
Saturday							
Parties	L H	35	50	am/pm		kitchen	
Parties	S H	30	35	am/pm		kitchen	
Social events	L H	120	120	eve	Occasional	kitchen	

Additional notes

1. Parish office at the front with a view of the entrance.
2. The new building should adjoin the church to produce optimum use of the facilities.
3. Glass doors allowing people to see into the church when they come for activities and vice versa.
4. More groups need refreshments preparation than a kitchen (warming kitchen) and an additional drinks machine would appeal to other groups.
5. Space would be used for coffee after church.
6. Any space may be locked off from the circulation area when any individual space is in use.
7. Budget is approximately £500,000.
8. If a children's group is in the main hall, it will be helpful (under the Children Act) for that group to have access to the toilets and no other. If small hall is also booked can one toilet, for example, the disabled accessible toilet, be available to that group's use?

Appendix 3
Church Hall Handbook

Contact for bookings and other inquiries: _____
Phone:
Office hours:[25]

Booking policy

1 All decisions with regard to booking the Church Hall are the responsibility of the Committee and are booked with the Hall Administrator.
2 Priority will be given to Church and Community Groups run by local people. [Optional]
3 Bookings will not be accepted from individuals or businesses for private profit. [Optional]
4 All bookings are subject to the guidelines of the Church Hall Management Committee.

Bookable spaces

1 Small hall on the first floor.
2 Large Hall for up to 250 people, with large stage area with off-street parking for six cars.
3 Kitchen.

---

25 This handbook is based on the *Purple Pack* from the Diocese of Southwark Communications Department.

Conditions of hire

1 The person making the application accepts full responsibility for the rooms booked.
2 Hiring agreements may only be made with people over 18 years of age.
3 The maximum number of people allowed is as follows:
   • Hall: 250
   • Small Hall: 35
4 The applicant will be given the following information at the time of booking:
   • Procedure in the event of a fire
   • Guidance on Health and Safety issues
   • Policy with regard to children on the premises
   • Code of practice
5 The Management Committee may waive or add to the Conditions and has the right to require the Hirer to make good or pay for any damage done to the building or its contents. The Committee will give reasons in writing if a booking application is refused for reasons other than that the space is already booked.

Payment

1 One-off Events pay £200 deposit on booking and a £50 deposit for cleaning. The deposits will be returned after the booking if there is no damage and the facilities are clean. The Hiring Fee must be paid in full at least 1 week before the booking. Deposits will be repaid one week after the booking if all the conditions of hire were complied with.
2 Regular Bookings are to be paid monthly in advance. If payment is not made prior to the first booked date, the booking is cancelled.
3 Hire Charges are as follows:
   • Large Hall: Monday to Friday 8.30 am to 5pm £15 per hour
   • Large Hall: Monday to Thursday 5pm to 10pm £20 per hour
   • Large Hall: Friday evening and weekends £35 per hour
   • Large Hall: £1,000 per full day for weekend events such as wedding receptions and parties

- Small Hall: Monday to Friday 8.30 am to 5pm £12 per hour
- Small Hall: Monday to Thursday 5pm to 10pm £15 per hour
- Small Hall: Friday evening and weekends £25 per hour
- Small Hall: £250 per full day for weekend events such as wedding receptions and parties
- Kitchen: (available only if booked in advance) the charge for use of the kitchen is an additional £5 per hour.

These charges are subject to annual review and are increased annually by at least the level of inflation.

Neighbours and nuisance

1 Because the Hall is in a residential area, noise must be kept at a reasonable volume, and complaints of nuisance will restrict the hirer's use of the premises on that and future occasions.
2 Complaints about noise and nuisance will be made direct to the users of the Hall and to the Caretaker.
3 All evening events will finish by 11pm when all music and public address systems will be switched off, and all users must leave by 11.30pm when the premises will be locked by the Caretaker. Please be quiet on leaving the building.
4 If users refuse to leave the premises or cause significant nuisance, noise or violence, or create difficulties for the Caretaker, the POLICE will be called.
5 The floor of the Hall must be swept/mopped clean before leaving at 11.30 pm, or the hirer forfeits the additional cleaning deposit. Tables and chairs are to be replaced as found and all rubbish removed and placed in the outside bins.
6 Any group putting up notices must:
   - USE THE NOTICEBOARDS and no other surfaces and
   - REMOVE ALL NOTICES at the end of the meeting/event

Equipment

1 Hirers may leave equipment on the premises only when given permission by the Caretaker and upon leaving a written list with the Caretaker.

2 Any equipment left on the premises is left entirely at the owner's risk.

3 Equipment that is the property of the Church Hall may not be removed from the building under any circumstances.

4 Hirers are expected to take care of Hall equipment and any problems or faults should be reported to the Caretaker immediately.

5 Hirers using equipment belonging to the Church Hall must not allow others to use that equipment without the permission of the Caretaker.

Code of Practice for general use of the building

1 All activities must be within the guidelines set by the Committee, especially with regard to Equal Opportunities, Health and Safety and the Children Act.

2 The Committee has a ZERO-TOLERANCE policy with regard to DRUGS and other illegal activity. Any hirer or hall user engaging in such illegal activity will be IMMEDIATELY barred from the premises and refused the right to make further bookings.

3 Hirers and users must ensure that their actions do not impinge on the health and safety of the staff, other users and the general public.

4 The Church is committed to combating racial discrimination and racist behaviour in all forms. This policy must be observed by all employees, community representatives and users of the building.

5 Applications to use the building are made to the Administrator in the first instance, using the standard booking form. Verbal bookings will not be accepted (even from church members).

6 All hirers and users must comply with the Bookings policy and conditions of the Church Hall.

7 The sale of alcohol is not permitted in the building.

8 Children under 16 years of age must be supervised at all times by a parent or by an accompanying person in charge of the child.

9 Users must not impinge on the privacy of staff or other users of the building.

10 Children must not be allowed to interfere with or operate electrical or fire-fighting equipment.

11 Fire roll registers must be kept when attending group meetings.
12 Fire exits must be kept clear and unlocked, and equipment must not be left obstructing the exits.
13 The building is alarmed. Please do not enter the building unless it is your booked time. In the event the alarm is triggered the Police will attend. Please contact the Caretaker if the alarm is triggered.
14 All due respect for neighbours must be given by users and hirers.
15 Cars should be parked so as not to block other vehicles' access. For safety reasons, cars may not be left in the car park while the owner is not in the building.

Insurance

1 The Church Hall carries third party indemnity for all users of the Centre, whether in paid employment, working as volunteers or as members of groups, who are injured as a result of the negligence of those responsible for the buildings. (*Check with the church's insurance provider.*)
2 Users leaving equipment or personal property at the Centre do so at their own risk. The Church Hall insurance does not cover loss of personal property or equipment.
3 Cars are parked on the property of the Church Hall at the owners' risk.

Responsibilities

1 It is the responsibility of group leaders to ensure that the conditions of all Codes of Practice, Procedure and Responsibilities are made familiar to ALL its members and adhered to at all times.
2 All members of the group must abide by the Conditions of Hire.
3 All members must be advised to take care in using the building and the equipment provided. The Caretaker must be notified immediately if parts of the building or equipment are thought to be dangerous or faulty.
4 Any accidents happening in the Hall must be reported to the Caretaker as soon as possible after the accident and the details entered in the accident book.

5 Group leaders must ensure that members are familiar with the procedure in the event of fire and have been issued with the Church Hall 'Procedure in the Event of Fire' leaflet.
6 Users must ensure that its members have signed a group registration book before the activity commences.
7 Each group must keep an up-to-date list of the names and addresses of volunteers supporting the group, which must be supplied to the Management Committee on request.
8 Groups are responsible for ensuring their own catering requirements are met.
9 All users must at all times ensure that their activities do not impinge on the safety or privacy of staff and other user groups.
10 Waste bins MUST BE EMPTIED AT THE END OF THE SESSION, by user groups, or before if necessary.

Child care

1 The Centre is not registered under the Children Act 1989. Under no circumstances, therefore, must a child be left at the Centre without her/his parent or carer for a period of more than two hours.
2 Parents and Carers are individually responsible for their own children's behaviour.
3 Gates must be placed at the entrance to the kitchen and kept shut when under-5s are on the premises.
4 All outside doors must remain shut when under-8s are on the premises.
5 Individual groups hiring the Hall must make their own further arrangements for compliance with the Children Act 1989.

Safety of children

1 Children under the age of 8 are NOT allowed in the kitchen AT ANY TIME.
2 Children between the ages of 8 and 16 must not be allowed in the kitchen unsupervised.
3 Children under the age of 16 are not allowed in the building unsupervised.

4 Children must not be allowed to climb on furniture or play with equipment. Parents and Carers must ensure that children are kept away from danger and their actions do not place risk on the safety of others using the building.

Health and safety

The Health and Safety at Work Act 1974 was passed to promote high standards of safety. As well as securing the health and safety and welfare of persons at work, the Act is designed to protect everyone using 'public' buildings.

General safety and accidents

1 Never climb on chairs or other furniture.
2 If the floor is wet for any reason, water must be mopped up immediately and a 'wet floor' sign displayed.
3 Do not store equipment that is thought to be unsafe without seeking the advice of the Caretaker.
4 Equipment used must be cleared and stored away after use.
5 Tablets, medicines and lotions must not be left lying around in the building.
6 ALL ACCIDENTS MUST BE RECORDED IN THE ACCIDENT BOOK AND REPORTED TO THE CARETAKER.

Smoking

1 No SMOKING is permitted in any part of the Hall.
2 People approaching the Hall while smoking should use outdoor ashtrays. Cigarette ends must not be placed in any bin containing paper or any other flammable material.

Gas

1 If you notice a smell of gas, check that all gas appliances are switched off. DO NOT SMOKE OR USE A NAKED FLAME; DO

NOT SWITCH ANY ELECTRIC APPLIANCE OR LIGHT ON
OR OFF AS THIS MAY IGNITE THE GAS.
2 Telephone the GAS EMERGENCY SERVICE ON _____.
  Or dial 999.
3 If practicable, assist members of your group to leave the building.
4 If a gas appliance appears faulty in any way the fault must be
  reported to the Caretaker immediately. DO NOT USE IT.
5 No GAS BOTTLES are permitted on the premises.[26]

Hygiene

1 Individuals suffering from sickness and diarrhoea should not handle
  food.
2 Hands should be washed prior to handling food and after using the
  toilets. A wash-hand basin is provided in the kitchen.
3 All cooking equipment, cooker, microwave, and sink should be left
  clean after use.
4 Not more than four people at one time should be in the kitchen.
5 Children under 8 are not allowed in the kitchen, under any circumstances.
6 No nappies to be placed in the kitchen bins. Please put them in the
  bin by the outside door.
7 Please leave toilets clean and tidy.
8 Mop up all spills immediately. This will prevent an accident occurring.

Electrical equipment

1 Do not use electrical equipment if you have any doubts about its
  safety.
2 Do not withdraw plugs by pulling on the cable.
3 Do not handle electrical equipment with wet hands.
4 All faulty equipment must be reported to the Management

---

26 Having bottled gas on your premises is extremely dangerous and may make your insurance cover void. Check with your insurer.

Committee, including frayed flexes, cracked, blackened, scorched sockets or plugs. Do not attempt to repair faulty equipment.

5 Do not overload the circuit, for example, by using multi-adaptors in wall sockets.

6 Do not trail loose cables under carpets or across floors.

7 Do not use portable electrical appliances in the toilets, even if they are plugged in outside the room.

8 Do not plug electrical equipment into ceiling light sockets.

9 Always switch off appliances after use and withdraw the plug.

Chemicals

1 All chemical and cleaning solutions must be locked away in a convenient and accessible place out of the reach of children.

2 Should an accident occur whereby someone is splashed in the eyes or on the skin with any chemical solution WASH WITH COLD WATER IMMEDIATELY. Continue to wash the eyes for at least 10 minutes. Seek medical assistance.

Fire

1 It is the responsibility of all users to ensure that all group members are familiar with the PROCEDURE IN THE EVENT OF FIRE leaflet.

2 Fire exits must never be obstructed, routes to fire exits must be clear at all times.

3 Check that doorways are kept free from obstructions.

PROCEDURE IN THE EVENT OF FIRE [sample notice]

If you discover a fire you should:

1 RAISE THE ALARM.

2 Ensure that all doors immediately surrounding the fire situation are CLOSED.

3 VACATE THE PREMISES.

4 Call the Fire Brigade by dialling 999.

5 When the Fire Brigade replies give direction to the building.

6 DO NOT replace the receiver until the Fire Officer has repeated the Address.

7 The building address is: _____

8 If you hear the Fire Alarm immediately escort the persons in your charge to safety outside the building.

9 Assemble at _____

10 When the people leaving the building assemble, take a roll call of those present and give this information to the person in charge.

11 Once the building has been evacuated UNDER NO CIRCUMSTANCES must the building be re-entered without the permission of the Fire Officer in charge.

12 CALL THE FIRE BRIGADE IMMEDIATELY TO EVERY FIRE OR SUSPICION OF FIRE.

13 Use fire-fighting equipment on small fires if necessary for evacuating the building. Do not attempt to extinguish large fires as this may endanger life.

SAMPLE BOOKING FORM – ONE-OFF BOOKINGS

Date of enquiry:_____

Date of Booking:_____

Rooms Booked: Small/Large Hall, Kitchen:_____

Time: from:_____ to _____

Total number of hours:_____

TOTAL COST (from arrival to set up, to departure after clearing up) using current hiring fees:_____

Returnable DEPOSIT PAID:_____

Name and address of hirer:_____

Phone:_____

I HAVE BEEN GIVEN INFORMATION ABOUT HEALTH AND SAFETY, PROCEDURES IN THE EVENT OF FIRE, CHILD PROTECTION AND CONDITIONS OF HIRE. I AGREE TO COMPLY WITH THEM.

I AM OVER 18.

I WILL ENSURE THAT MY GROUP FINISHES ON TIME AND THAT LOCKING UP CAN HAPPEN AT THE AGREED TIME.

Signature of applicant:_____

One copy is given to Hirer and one copy is retained by the Centre.

SAMPLE BOOKING FORM – REGULAR BOOKINGS

Group name:_____

Organizer:_____

Address:_____

Telephone:_____

Rooms required:_____

Day/s:_____

Arrival time:_____

Leaving time (after clear up):_____

Date of first meeting:_____

Expected number at sessions:_____

Will group meet in school holidays:_____

Hourly rate of room/s:_____

Cost per session:_____

I HAVE BEEN GIVEN THE CENTRE HANDBOOK WHICH I WILL MAKE AVAILABLE TO MY GROUP AND AGREE TO KEEP TO ALL THE CONDITIONS AND GUIDELINES IN THE HANDBOOK.

I AGREE THAT MY GROUP WILL PAY FOR ITS HIRING THE CHURCH HALL MONTHLY IN ADVANCE AND THAT FAILURE TO PAY FORFEITS THE BOOKINGS.

Signature of Organizer:_____

Date:_____

One copy of this form is given to the Organizer and one is held on the Church Hall files.

Appendix 4

Elements of a Contract of Employment

Part One – required by law to be stated in full

Name[27] of the employer and employee:_____

Job title and summary of duties:_____

Place of work:_____

Date of start of continuous employment:_____

Rate of pay and interval of payment:_____

How contract may be terminated:_____

Normal hours of work and any flexi- or variable-time arrangements:_____

Statement of Trade Union recognition or not:_____

Holiday and holiday pay entitlements:_____

Part Two – to be stated but not necessarily in the contract

Grievance procedure.

Disciplinary procedure.

---

27 This Appendix is based on *The Project Worker*, Alison Peacock, The Church Urban Fund, 2000.

Pension arrangements.

Sickness arrangements and pay during sickness.

Part Three – sensible but not required and may be separate from the contract

Maternity pay, leave agreement and any agreed extensions of leave.

Contractual maternity leave (legal minimum).

Parental leave agreement.

Other leave, such as compassionate leave.

Variations on the contract.

Part-time employees (noting that in most cases they have the same rights as full-time employees).

Equal Opportunities.

Health & Safety policies.

Probationary period and process of confirming the appointment.

Signatures of the employee and employer (essential)

Resources

General
Building Preservation Trusts, Heritage Lottery Fund, 1999.
The Charities Act and the PCC, Church House Publishing, 2001.
Charity Accounts 2001, Charity Commission, 2001.
Church Extensions and Adaptations, Council for the Care of Churches, 1996.
Conservation Plans for Historic Places, Heritage Lottery Fund, 1998.
Creating and Managing New Projects, Alan Lawrie, Directory of Social Change, 1996.
Discipline at Work, Advisory Conciliation and Arbitration Service, 1987.
Getting Organised, Christine Holloway and Shirley Otto, Bedford Square Press, 1985.
Hall Management for both Mission and Money, Woolwich Area Mission Team, Diocese of Southwark, 1998.
The Health and Safety Handbook, Al Hinde and Charlie Kavanagh, Directory of Social Change, 1998.
Making Changes to a Listed Church, The General Synod, Church of England, 1999.
Managing People, Gill Taylor and Christine Thornton, Directory of Social Change, 1995.
Managing Your Community Building, Peter Hudson, Community Matters, 2000.
New Work in Historic Places of Worship, English Heritage, 2003.
A Practical Guide to PAYE, Kate Sayer, Directory of Social Change, 1995.
The Project Worker, Alison Peacock, Church Urban Fund, 2000.
The Purple Pack for Planning Projects, Diocese of Southwark Communications Department.
Redecorating your Church, Council for the Care of Churches, 1986.
Responsible Care of Churchyards, Council for the Care of Churches, 1993.
Safe and Sound: A Guide to Church Security, Geoffrey Crago and Graham Jeffery, Church House Publishing, 1996.
Village and Community Halls, National Lottery distributing bodies, 1996.

Access plans
Easy Access to Historic Properties, English Heritage, 1995.

Widening the Eye of the Needle: Access to Church Buildings for People with Disabilities, John Penton, Church House Publishing, 2001.

Contacts
Through the Roof, PO Box 178, Cobham, Surrey, KT11 1YN. www.throughtheroof.org
The Heritage Lottery Fund.

Health and Safety
Health and Safety Executive leaflets
Riddor Explained: Reporting of Injuries, Diseases, and Dangerous Occurrences Regulations
Stating your Business: Guidance on Preparing a Health & Safety Policy Document for Small Firms
Basic Advice on First Aid at Work
Manual Handling: A short Guide for Employers
Employers' Liability (Compulsory Insurance) Act 1969
Managing Health and Safety: Five Steps to Success
Health and Safety Training: What You Need to Know
Officewise
First Aid at Work: Your Questions Answered
COSHH: A Brief Guide to the Regulations (Control of Substances Hazardous to Health Regulations 2002)
Electrical Safety and You
Five Steps to Risk Assessment
The Health and Safety executive can be accessed on the web at www.hse.gov.uk

See also www.churchsafety.org.uk

Care and maintenance
Church House Publishing
The Churchwarden's Year: A Calendar of Church Maintenance
Church Log Book
Church Property Register (Terrier and Inventory)
The Care of Church Plate (and many other small booklets on aspects of caring for church fabric and contents)
A Guide to Church Inspection and Repair

A Guide for the Quinquennial Inspection of Churches, Diocese of Birmingham, 1993.
How to Look After Your Church, Council for the Care of Churches, Church Information Office, 1970–.

The Joint Repair Scheme of English Heritage and the Heritage Lottery Fund produces an outline for a schedule of planned maintenance.

Index

Abuses in the workplace 142
Access: increasing 33
Adaptation 58
Administration 71, 133
Additional uses 56
Adviser on repairs 44
Aims 15
Alcohol in churches 103
Alterations to buildings 49
Alterations, explaining the need 95
Annual inspection 37
Architect 105
Architect and design team 105
Architects and changing them 46
Architect's certificate 114
Architectural history 14
Architectural oversight 80
Arson 28

Begging 89
Bookings to avoid 73
Boundaries 88
Brief 100, 108
Brief preparation chart 146
Building projects, major 95

Caretaker 134

Cashflow 117
Change of use 56
Character (new building) 101
Church hall handbook 150
Commercial activities 62ff
Community Projects 82
Computer workstation 140
Conflict 141
Conservation 48
Conservation plan 48
Construction (Design and management) 118
Contract of employment elements 162
Cost changes 117

Data safety 31
Delays 116
Design detailed 109, 112
Design team 105
Diocesan Advisory Committee 52
Directions 87
Disabled accessible facilities 100
Dismissal 142

Employer's responsibilities 135
Electrical safety 25, 26

Equal opportunities 136

Faculty jurisdiction 52
Faculty 57
Fee levels: letting 74
Fees: architect and design team
    105, 107, 112
Financial structure 64
Fire risks 26
Fire safety policy 28
Fire damage control 29
Fixtures and fittings 117
Funds – processing 111

Gas heaters 25
Gutter inspection 38

Halls, explaining the need 96
Hazardous substances 30
Heads of terms 78
Health and Safety 23
Heating risks 27
Historic buildings and
    alterations 102

Indemnity 118
Inspection annual 37
Inspection cycle 39ff
Insurance 118
Inventory 37

Job descriptions 132

Leadership 128
Leases long-term 76
Leases: heads of terms 78
Leasing 71
Legal consents 110
Legal issues 59

Letting 71
Letting to families and private
    events 74
Licensing 102
Listed churches 54
Location 101
Log book 36
Longevity 100

Maintenance 36
Managing people 125
Managing buildings 125
Managing construction projects
    103
Managing specialised activities
    65
Mechanical and electrical
    engineer 106
Mission statement 15
Modifications 116

Need assessment 95
New uses 66, 125
New uses: finance 66
New uses: staff time 67
New works in buildings 49

Office work space 30
Outside facilities 101
Ownership 101

Partnership 68
PAYE 138
Place of safety 38
Planning permission 62, 101
Practical completion 115
Problems on building projects
    115

Professional indemnity 118
Project management 103
Public safety 31
Purpose 15

Quantity surveyor 104, 106
Quinquennial inspection report
    44

Recruiting 137
Redundancy 142
Rent increases 81
Repairs 43
Resources 166
Restoration 48
Review 85
Risk analysis 117, 119, 145
Risk assessment for health and
    safety 23ff
Risks, maintenance and building
    works 30

Safety of data 31
Safety and general public 31
Salvage 29
Scaffolding 115
Schedule of new facilities 58
Scheduling use 71
Security 86
Service charge 79
Signs 87
Smoking 27
Snagging 124
Space for mission and ministry
    77

Specification 115
Staff meetings 128
Staff skills 67
Staff structure 131
Staff time 58, 67
Staff welfare 139
Statement of need 56
Statement of significance 56
Story of the church 14
Strategy 18
Structural engineer 106
Supervision 141
Surprises 116
Sustainability 82, 84

Tenants 79
Tendering for work 112
Terrier 36
Trading 61

Utilities 80

Value Added Tax 60
Value to local people 13
Values statement 17
Visitors 86
Visitors and attracating them 90
Visitor behaviour 88
Visitor health and safety 90
Visitors and security 86
Volunteers 132

Water drainage 39
Welcome 87
Working environment 135